Kim Williams'
COOKBOOK & COMMENTARY

Kim Williams'
COOKBOOK & COMMENTARY

A Seasonal Celebration of Good Food For Mind & Body

Knight-Ridder Press

Tucson, Arizona

Published by Knight-Ridder Press,
A Division of HPBooks, Inc.
P.O. Box 5367
Tucson, AZ 85703

Library of Congress Cataloging in Publication Data

Williams, Kim.
    Kim Williams' cookbook & commentary

    Reprint. Originally published: Missoula, Mont.:
Bitterroot Educational Resources, © 1983.
    Includes index.
    1. Cookery. 2. Cookery (Natural foods) 3. Cookery
(Wild foods) I. Title. II Title: Kim Williams' cookbook
& commentary. III Title: cookbook & commentary.
TX715.W7254 1987 641.5 86-82242
ISBN: 0-89586-518-1

Printed in U.S.A.

10   9   8   7   6   5   4   3   2

1st Printing

*This book is dedicated to the world
and everything in it,
of which you and I are a part.*

I want to thank Candace Crosby, Linda Smith and Judy Smith of Bitterroot Educational Resources for the idea and design of this book and for gently nudging me through more and more additions until we had a book twice as big as I thought I could do. I want to thank my husband, Mel, for being himself—an oak tree, calm and strong.

Table of Contents

About This Book . . . .

Sometimes I think I am the reincarnation of a horse. I dearly love seeds, grains, nuts. I eat huge salads of greens fresh from the fields. I forage for overripe fruit falling off the trees.

But life is a paradox. When my mother makes Hungarian *Kalács*, which is a Christmas bread, I'm right there, eating half of it. White flour and white sugar and eggs. But *Kalács* is my childhood. When I sit in my mother's kitchen I'm back in my childhood — which wasn't all that great. It was during the Great Depression. But it was my childhood.

I once weighed one hundred sixty pounds. Now I weigh one hundred twenty-five and I've stayed there for thirty-five years. I changed my way of eating and my way of living. My husband is seventy-three. He climbs mountains with a forty-five pound backpack and bakes his own whole wheat trail bread. Luckily, because I am no great bread baker. There are people who bake perfect bread. My life is not perfection.

Today I don't eat a quarter of the meat I used to. I still get all the protein I need — in fact, more than I need, but I'm varying the sources of the protein. I eat moderate amounts of meat, cheese and eggs. I eat beans, peas and lentils. I eat fruits and vegetables. I eat bread.

If the world were perfect — if I were perfect — I would eat one hundred percent whole wheat bread all the time, made from freshly milled wheat. If you have ever tasted bread made from flour milled that same day you will know what I mean when I say good bread needs no butter. We could live on that kind of bread, the staff of life.

But of course the world isn't perfect. I'm not perfect, you're not perfect. We will eat Danish, doughnuts, chocolate chip cookies, white bread. Right in this book I have a recipe for Indian Fry Bread and it's made with white flour. It's because I believe in rituals, in ritualistic eating. My parents were Hungarian. My husband and I lived in South America for eighteen years. A Chilean *Pastel de Choclo* is part of me. I went out of my way during a trip down the Amazon to eat Brazilian *Feijoada*, a very motley dish of black beans and many very peculiar parts of the pig; but it's a national dish and I had to taste it. I respect traditions, customs.

1

I'm also willing to break with tradition. I have in many of my eating habits. But Hungarian *Kalács* is made with white flour. South American *Empanadas* are made with white flour. Indian Fry Bread is made with white flour. To use white flour and white sugar in celebration is one thing, to stuff our stomachs with it three times a day is an entirely different matter.

The old expression "If I'd known you were coming I'd have baked a cake" — wherever it came from — has wisdom. In the days of scarcity, white flour and sugar were a luxury. The person baking the cake was offering a great gift. When my Hungarian mother made *Kalács* during the Depression she was using scarce, luxury-type ingredients. Even then she didn't put frosting on cake or cookies. Maybe that's why to this day I don't care for frosting on cake or cookies. It's too much sugar and fat for me.

I make cookies with half the sugar that is in ordinary recipes. I make granola with half the oil and half the honey most recipes call for. I tell people "I'm making granola, not candy." I am not a fanatic about sugar versus honey. I think honey is better for us, but I think the number one priority is to cut down on all types of sugars. I get most of my sweetening needs from fruits, vegetables, nuts, grains. You'd be surprised how much sugar there is in baked winter squash. I eat my squash with no sugar added, no honey either.

I say yes to sugar when it is part of a celebration. I even say yes to coffee. One cup of coffee, like one glass of wine, to celebrate the breaking of bread among friends. My point is we have to learn — and to teach our children — the difference between basic food and everyday existence, and the celebrations which don't happen every day. Sugar and coffee and wine have been made everyday items, every hour for some!

Spring is only once a year, summer is once a year, life goes through fall into winter. We have to learn to deal with everyday life. I cook beans in winter, without sugar, without molasses. I make wheatberry soup. And garlic soup, from real chickens. When a blizzard comes I run up and down the basement stairs. I bend and stretch. I serve lean cookies and herb tea. I try to hang on to reality.

Spring is
Wild and Green

Watercress Salad

Like a bear coming out of hibernation and making its first meal on wild greens, so I start my eating year with a watercress salad. It's my spring tonic in two ways: the high vitamin and mineral value makes it what I consider a natural vitamin pill; and when I'm out collecting watercress I'm going through one of my most important spring rituals—searching for spring. People who live in the seasons, as I do, have to do things in their proper order or the year will never go along properly.

While I'm hiking along a mountain stream looking for watercress, I'm also looking for the first redwinged blackbird in a cattail marsh. I'm looking for the first sagebrush buttercup. I'm listening for the high wild honking of Canada geese heading north. I bring all this home when I bring the watercress home.

Of course you don't need to go out in the snow and ice and find your own watercress. You can buy it in the market. The plant is the same, *Rorippa nasturtium-aquaticum.* If you do use wild watercress—or any other wild edible plant I mention in this book—please read my ten rules for eating wild plants safely.

2 cups watercress, tips and leaves only

1 cup celery, cut in short strips

1 avocado, peeled and sliced

4 tablespoons French Dressing

Wash watercress. If necessary, soak it in a water-purifying solution. (See Rule 10.) Rinse well. Dry on a paper towel.

Toss watercress, celery and avocado with French Dressing. Serve on lettuce leaves.

French Dressing

¼ cup vinegar

¾ cup oil

¼ teaspoon salt

¼ teaspoon black pepper

¼ teaspoon paprika

¼ teaspoon dry mustard

¼ teaspoon powdered oregano

Place all ingredients in a jar and shake well. Store, covered, in a cool place.
This makes one cup.

Ten Rules For Eating Wild Plants Safely

1. Do not eat anything that you cannot positively identify. There are poisonous plants that you must avoid.

2. Be prepared to study. There is no shortcut to learning about edible wild plants. The best way to learn is to have a guide who takes you on field trips. The next best way is to take a course. The third way is to buy books and study on your own.

3. Learn the scientific names. There are too many plants called pigweed, chickweed, wild spinach, etc.

4. Learn the plant in all stages of growth: first shoots of spring, flowering plant, fruit stage, dry winter stage.

5. Start with one or two. You cannot hope to learn all the edible plants in one season.

6. Know what part of the plant is edible and when it is edible. For instance, the fruit of the elderberry is edible when ripe but toxic when green. The green twigs are toxic at all times.

7. Use recipes. In order to enjoy wild plants you have to prepare them properly.

8. Eat just a sample the first time. Our Twentieth Century stomachs are not accustomed to pioneer fare. Also, different people react differently to new foods.

9. Watch out for contamination. This could be sprays, fertilizers or animal wastes.

10. One standard purifying solution for bacterial contamination, used to purify drinking water and also for soaking wild greens, is eight drops household bleach to one gallon water. Let stand one hour before using. In the case of greens, soak one hour.

I have a rule 11. It has nothing to do with safety. It has to do with being thoughtful. Every year I get a phone call like this: "I just picked a bushel basket of chokecherries. What'll I do with them?" I always say, or I feel like saying, "Go put them right back on the bushes." We shouldn't go through the outdoors like Attila the Hun. Take only a little. The birds and wild animals need their share.

These ten rules are reprinted from *Eating Wild Plants* by Kim Williams, by permission of Mountain Press Publishing Company, Missoula, Montana.

Hominy and Watercress Frittata

Hominy is whole grains of corn that were dried and then softened by soaking, often in solutions made from wood ashes, and then cooked. It is not as nutritious as sweet corn because the hull—and sometimes the germ—has been removed. However, I find it a good variation. Since it is mature corn, it is not as sugar-sweet as sweet corn.

In the following recipe the starchy hominy is combined with bland eggs and milk, then livened up by tangy watercress. Cooked kale, chopped fine, can be used in place of the watercress. Kale has a tangy taste also. I like this dish for breakfast.

1½ tablespoons butter

1 cup watercress, stems removed

2 cups canned hominy, drained (save liquid for soup)

4 eggs

4 tablespoons milk

½ teaspoon salt

dash of pepper

1 tablespoon chopped parsley

Chop the watercress coarsely. In a heavy skillet heat the butter. Add watercress and stir-fry 1 minute. Add hominy. Do not stir.

Remove the skillet from the fire and cover it so the hominy will warm through gently. Beat eggs with milk, using a wire whisk or fork. Add salt and pepper. Reheat the skillet.

Pour egg mixture on top of the watercress and hominy. Cook over low heat until eggs are custard consistency, lifting cooked parts with pancake turner to enable uncooked mixture to reach hot skillet. Turn off heat and cover the skillet. Let it sit 2 minutes to firm the top. Sprinkle with parsley. Cut in wedges and serve on hot plates.

Four servings.

What Is A Spring Tonic?

If someone said to you, "What is a spring tonic?" you might say, "It's grandma's sulfur and molasses." By the end of winter people felt rundown, out of energy. Actually what they were out of is vitamins. In the days before supermarkets and year-round fresh fruit and vegetables, people simply ran out of vitamins by the end of the winter. They were living on bread, potatoes and salt pork. An orange was something you got at Christmas in your stocking. I really don't know why the tonic was sulfur and molasses.

I can see the molasses part. In the government bulletin on the nutritive value of foods, molasses — especially blackstrap molasses — is listed as having a considerable amount of vitamins and minerals. My husband drinks a blackstrap molasses milkshake for lunch. Now, don't picture a high calorie ice cream milkshake. No. His is low-fat milk with blackstrap molasses.

Another spring tonic is fresh greens. Watercress, dandelion greens, curly dock. It's too early for any of these, it's true. I'm buying my watercress in the store and eating kale and mustard greens instead of the wild greens I'm only dreaming of so far.

I do have one kind of fresh greens in my kitchen. Those are sprouts. I sprout alfalfa seeds in my own kitchen and after the sprouts are two inches long I put the glass jar in the window and let the sun turn the sprouts green. Then you have chlorophyll and you have the same kind of vitamins you would have in dandelion greens freshly pulled from your lawn.

Alfalfa sprouts are becoming very popular. They can take the place of lettuce in both salads and sandwiches. Have you tried a sandwich of avocado, cream cheese and alfalfa sprouts, on whole wheat bread? It's delicious. And very healthful.

Radish seeds sprout easily too and they turn nice and green. They add a slightly peppery taste, like radishes. You could sprout parsley seeds too, celery — oh, dozens of seeds.

Of course sprouting seeds is an art. You have to do it right. Rinsing is the important part. You have to rinse the seeds two or three times a day with lukewarm water.

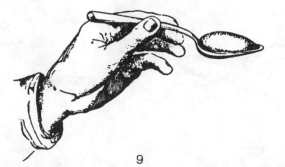

You can buy the sprouts ready to eat in a grocery store. Even supermarkets carry two or three kinds. But the fresher you get them the more vitamins they will have. And that's what a spring tonic is all about — something to perk up your motor.

And here's where I come to what I think is the best spring tonic of all — to get out of the house and go searching for spring. In the slush and snow, before one leaf has broken out of its bud. There are signs. One patch of green grass on the sunny side of the house, an imaginary movement under the leaf mulch covering the crocus.

If a neighbor sees you staring intently at an absolutely bare piece of ground, smile and say, "I'm searching for spring." Maybe you'll even help it along.

Dandelion Bud Omelet

Your neighbors will love you if you make this recipe because by picking the dandelion buds you are preventing them from flowering and going to seed, and everyone knows what happens to dandelion seeds. They blow into the neighbors' yards and start new young plants there.

1 ½ tablespoons butter

1 cup dandelion buds

¼ cup minced onion

4 eggs

3 tablespoons milk

1 tablespoon chopped parsley

¼ teaspoon salt

In a heavy skillet heat the butter. Add dandelion buds and onion. Saute 3 minutes. Remove dandelion buds and onion from skillet.

In a large bowl beat the eggs with milk. Add parsley and salt. Pour mixture into hot skillet. Sprinkle dandelion buds and onion on top. Cook over low heat for 3 or 4 minutes, lifting edges of omelet with fork or spatula so uncooked egg can reach the hot skillet.

Just before serving, fold half the omelet over the other half.

Four servings.

Eunice Brown's Dandelion Salad

Ten minutes from earth to table—that's how fresh a dandelion salad can be. Can you imagine how full of vitamins and minerals that salad is?

In the old days the dandelion was used as a medicine. The botanical name, *Taraxacum officinale*, means officially recognized as a remedy for internal disorders.

In the days before year-round fresh produce was available people often fell ill in great numbers during late winter and early spring. Oldtime herb doctors squeezed the juice out of freshly dug dandelion plants and gave it to the sick. They also told the patient to eat the first new leaves. The oldtime doctors didn't know the terms vitamins and minerals, but they knew that there is something in certain plants that acts as a tonic.

"But dandelion greens are so bitter," you will say. The secret is to pick them in early spring, before the yellow flowers appear. Look for the plants that grow in a shady spot in good soil. I tell my students to pick dandelions under a flatbed truck on the north side of the barn.

Many people would like to try a dandelion salad but they don't find a recipe in their cookbook. Here is Eunice Brown's version of the old-fashioned wilted dandelion greens salad. Everyone knows Eunice Brown but I have the honor of living across the street from her. Last Saturday she came over with a plateful of the salad—hot, ready to eat.

Here is the rest of the menu that goes with the dandelion salad, put in Eunice Brown's words: "You need a freshly caught trout. Don't waste anything. Take the fish eggs and fish livers and cook them with wild onions."

This is a menu from the days when Eunice and her husband went out camping—and took their canning equipment with them. Can you imagine canning and processing fish while out camping?

They also canned wild raspberries, thimbleberries and strawberries. Around the edges of these projects, right there in the wild, Eunice made hot biscuits and cornbread. And she's still here to tell the tale at 87, and spry enough to drive her own car and invite twenty-five people to lunch.

1 quart very young tender dandelion leaves

3 tablespoons chopped green onion tops

2 strips bacon

1 egg (slightly beaten)

⅓ cup thin cream

¼ teaspoon sugar

1 tablespoon vinegar

Wash leaves and drain. Pat dry on paper towel, then shred finely. Place in a bowl.

Cut bacon in small pieces and cook in a skillet until crisp. Drain off almost all of the bacon grease. Add the egg, cream, sugar, salt and vinegar to the skillet. Stir over low heat until thick. The dressing will look curdled, but that is the way it should look.

Pour the hot dressing over the shredded greens. To serve, empty the salad on a warm platter. Place the chopped green onion tops in a ring around the mound of salad.

The poet William Blake saw the whole world in a grain of sand. I see it in the dandelion: to spray or not to spray. Is this dandelion an enemy? Should I hate it? A man once said that to me as he was spraying furiously, "I hate dandelions!"

Our ancestors brought the dandelion from Europe because they wanted it here. Its yellow flowers reminded them of home. And they ate it. If we didn't have supermarkets with year-round fresh produce we'd be outside in March praying for a little old dandelion. With all that vitamin C to cure our end-of-winter letdown, the dandelion is a spring tonic.

Purslane Tabouli Salad

I think of tabouli as a Lebanese potato salad. You don't have potatoes but you have a starchy base; in this case, cracked wheat. The type of cracked wheat used is bulgur, which is cooked, dried cracked wheat. You can make the tabouli without cooking the bulgur any more. Just soak it in warm water until the crunchiness is gone. Then add vegetables, seasoning, oil and lemon juice.

Just as with potato salad, the variations are endless. You can make tabouli a whole meal with complete protein by adding the right vegetables. Wheat is complemented by any of the legume family. I sometimes add chick peas, sprouted lentils, or soybean sprouts to my tabouli.

Purslane is a ''weed'' in your garden but it can be a nutritious food. It is especially rich in iron.

1 cup bulgur wheat

1½ cups water

2 cups chopped purslane, leafy tips only

¼ cup minced green onion

1 clove garlic, minced

1 teaspoon chopped fresh mint (optional)

¼ cup grated carrot

¼ cup chopped parsley

3 tablespoons oil

3 tablespoons lemon juice

1 large tomato, diced

lettuce leaves

Add the bulgur to water in a saucepan. Bring to a boil. Remove from fire, cover and allow it to sit 1 hour. Chill.

Add purslane, onion, garlic, mint, carrot, parsley, oil and lemon juice. Mix. Place in bowl, cover, and refrigerate at least 1 hour.

Just before serving add diced tomato. Mix. Serve on lettuce leaves.

Four servings.

Poke And The Rundown Farm

I received a letter from a schoolteacher in Pennsylvania. "We live on a rundown farm," the letter said. Right away I wanted to fly out of the window, go to Pennsylvania, and walk on that rundown farm. People who eat wild plants love rundown farms. That's where you find your dinner. Or your lunch. Especially in spring.

When the last of your canned food is gone, the rootcellar is empty, and before the garden produces anything, that's when you go out in the meadows and fields and look for what's coming up.

What does this schoolteacher find on her farm in Pennsylvania? Dandelions, of course. Nice big fat ones. And wild daylilies. You can eat the tubers, the new shoots and the flowers. She also finds Jerusalem artichokes, which grow both in gardens and in the wild.

The fourth plant the woman mentioned (her name is Clemence) is the famous poke. Some people call it poke weed, others call it poke salad. This plant is very special to me because I've never eaten it. We don't have it in the Rocky Mountains. It grows in the east from Maine to Florida, and west to the Great Plains.

Now I like the idea that I've never eaten this delicacy It gives me something to look forward to. Everyone should have something delectable to look forward to.

I know poke is going to be delectable when I get around to eating it. A neighbor of mine is from Kentucky and he bubbled over when I asked him about poke. "I tell you," he said, "you go out in early spring and you cut the new shoots of poke just like you cut asparagus. Then you find some bits of salt pork and cook that poke along with the salt pork. Now that's a dish fit to eat."

I know the fruit of the poke plant is not edible. In fact it is toxic. You can get sick from it. But many plants are like that. You have to know what part of the plant to eat. Poke is eaten new and fresh and young, right out of the ground.

Clemence freezes poke for a winter salad, she says, along with cherry tomatoes. Clemence also freezes lambs quarter and purslane. Her letter says, "We are discovering new ways of using the many untapped riches of our somewhat unproductive farm."

She doesn't really mean her farm is unproductive. A rundown farm is never unproductive. Think of the wild strawberries she's going to have. And the mushrooms. "We have a Russian friend," she says, "who's an expert." That's the only way to pick wild mushrooms. It's too risky otherwise.

Oh, a rundown farm is a gold mine. I'm going exploring in an old orchard tomorrow, for dandelion greens and chickweed and Jerusalem artichokes. No poke, but that's OK. There's poke in my future.

Wild Asparagus - Morel Mushroom Stir-Fry

The ritual of going out to look for wild asparagus is as important as the moon and the tides. Well, it's probably connected with the moon and the tides—and the sun and the rain and the wind. Wild asparagus is part of spring; it's a celebration.

But if you come home emptyhanded, it doesn't matter at all. You've had your hike and now you can stop by a market and buy some asparagus. (I do that too. I think I've taught too many classes. My students find all the wild asparagus. Well, there's a certain justice in that.)

Wild asparagus is exactly the same as garden asparagus or supermarket asparagus. It's all *Asparagus officinalis*, and you can use any kind you want in this recipe.

Morel mushrooms—or any wild mushroom—should be hunted only by people who know how to identify wild mushrooms. "Don't poison yourself for sixty cents," I tell my students. "That's all a can of mushrooms costs in the store."

But if you are willing to study and work (see my ten rules for eating wild plants safely on page 7), oh, the joy of finding morel mushrooms! I jump up and down and screech and holler. It's an ancient joy, going right back to the time when our ancestors lived in caves and plucked something here and something there and said, "Eureka! Today I dine!"

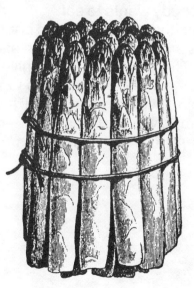

You can eat both wild asparagus and morels raw but they are also good stir-fried. Stir-frying is one of the best ideas to be incorporated into our American way of life. We should have done it centuries ago.

Stir-frying means you just barely grease or oil the skillet (a wok, of course, is the proper utensil but any heavy pot will do) and then you very briefly cook the food. You preserve almost all the vitamins and minerals this way. And you don't mush the vegetables into a glop that nobody wants to eat.

Actually neither the asparagus nor the mushrooms are the truly nutritious parts of this recipe. The broccoli and tofu give you the most for your money. Broccoli is a top-of-the-list vegetable. A serving of broccoli has far more vitamin A, vitamin C, calcium, potassium and iron than asparagus.

Mushrooms are really very low in nutritive value. Eat them for flavor and for fun, but don't count them as adding to your health.

Tofu does add to your health. It's practically a staple for vegetarians. It's a kind of soft cheese made from soybeans. It's easily digested, high in protein, and one pound can be made from only six ounces of soybeans. Guess how many pounds of cattle feed (soybeans and grains) it takes to yield one pound of beef? According to the book *Diet for a Small Planet* by Frances Moore Lappe it takes sixteen pounds. You can see why people say, "Instead of passing the soybeans and grain through cattle let's just eat the beans and grain."

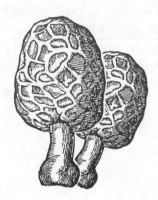

½ **pound tofu**

1 tablespoon soy sauce

1 tablespoon lemon juice

¼ **pound morel mushrooms (you can use store-bought mushrooms)**

1 small bunch broccoli

4 - 6 stalks wild asparagus (tame will do too)

1 cup celery

1 medium onion

1 tablespoon oil

Cut tofu into one inch cubes. Marinate the tofu in soy sauce and lemon juice, turning cubes until they are evenly seasoned. This takes at least one half hour.

If the morel mushrooms are clean, do not wash them. Wipe them with a paper towel. Discard any that are wormy. Cut into bite-size pieces.

Cut broccoli into bite-size pieces. Chop the asparagus into one inch pieces. Chop the celery diagonally into small pieces. Cut the onion in small slices.

Heat the oil in a wok or heavy skillet. (It should be hot enough that a cube of bread foams when dropped in it.) Stir-fry onion and celery 3 minutes. Add mushrooms and broccoli and stir-fry 2 minutes. Add asparagus. Stir-fry another 2 minutes. Turn heat off or very low.

Place tofu on top of the vegetables and pour any marinade that was not absorbed over the tofu. Cover the wok or skillet and let stand 2 minutes to allow the tofu to warm through.

Serve on steamed brown rice.

Four servings.

Could We Have Flowering Roadsides Again?

I'm walking in a wild strawberry patch along a highway. I'm dreaming of a strawberry shortcake. But I'm worried. Suppose the county spray truck comes by. What will happen to the strawberries? If there is some fruit will I dare eat it?

I've been doing a lot of thinking about roadsides lately. Is it necessary to spray them? Maybe with the high rate of unemployment we could hire people to cut the weeds. That's what they did in South America. We lived along the Pan American Highway in Chile. I almost wrote a letter once to a lady in New England. She had an article in the *New Yorker* gently lamenting the loss of the flowering roadsides in New England. The phone comany was spraying, the highway crews were spraying — everyone was spraying the roadsides.

I almost wrote to her. I wanted to say, "Please come down immediately. The flowering roadsides are still here." What a sight it was to drive along the Pan American Highway in southern Chile. California poppies as bright as gold covering the roadbanks. The story is the seeds were imported from California. A lady rode the train from Santiago to the coast — two and one half hours — and flung seeds out of the window. I read the other day that California poppies now have to be protected in California. Is that possible? Is it possible that the California poppy will survive in Chile instead of California? It's because they don't spray the roadsides in Chile.

Red poppies are there too. They escape from people's gardens and just bloom away for all the passersby to see. And blue vetch. Oh, how that blue vetch climbs over bushes and fences! And wild fennel, smelling like anise for miles. It's so tall you can play hide and seek in it. Think how happy the birds are to have those lovely thickets. Wild roses. Miles of wild roses. The air is so sweet you can think back in mid-winter and remember summer. It almost hurts to remember — it's so beautiful.

I discovered a rare red nasturtium once. It was climbing down a bank where an irrigation ditch ran. The Chilean nasturtiums are the ancestor of our cultivated nasturtiums. This one was rare even in Chile. I stumbled on it when we stopped the car for a rest stop. It's a pleasure to make a rest stop when you have flowering roadsides like gardens of Eden.

I remember the wild daisies — white daisies as far as you could see. Meadows filled with them. There were always cows grazing in those meadows. "Like an ad for Borden's milk," I said to Mel. A black and white cow in a meadow filled with white daisies.

Orange and yellow lilies. So many lilies country children picked them and sold them in the market. Wild fuchsia. Another ancestor. Small flowers on large bushes. That's its natural habitat — the southern end of South America.

The other day I read that somewhere in the United States a group of garden clubs are replanting the roadsides in their area. They're making a campaign. "Bring back the scythe," they said. "We don't mind if you cut our plants when they get old and stringy. But let them bloom in spring and early summer." A splendid idea. Wouldn't it be marvelous to drive along and instead of one straight manicured lawn from Maine to California, we could see poppies and daisies and lupine and foxglove — a rainbow of colors that changed from state to state? How's that for a project for local clubs? Bring back the flowering roadsides. Color the highways from Maine to California.

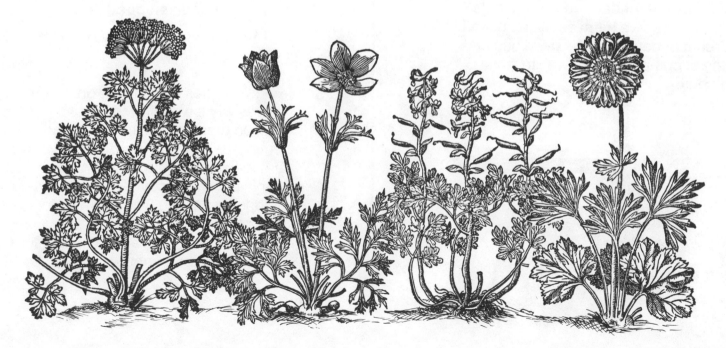

Potato and Nettle Soup

Stinging nettle (*Urtica dioica*) will sting you, but you can take your revenge by eating it. You will need leather gloves and a knife to gather it but after it is cooked the stinging quality disappears.

The plant has to be used when very young, only five to six inches tall. The flavor is delicate and the nutritional value is high: all the vitamin A and C you need for a day in one hundred grams of the nettle leaves, plus five and one half grams of protein, which is unusually high for a green plant.

Young nettles are tender and require little cooking. You can serve them as plain cooked greens. Cream of nettle soup is delicious and a nettle omelet compares very well to a spinach omelet.

2 cups stinging nettles *

2 cups diced potato

1 cup sliced onions

1 teaspoon salt

3 cups water

2 tablespoons butter

1 tablespoon flour

1 cup milk

dash of turmeric

1 tablespoon snipped chives

1 tablespoon chopped parsley

Pick nettles with gloves on. Wear rubber gloves while washing them.

Drop them into boiling water and simmer for 1 minute. The stinging quality is now gone. Drain and set aside.

In a pot with a cover, simmer the potatoes, onions and salt in 3 cups water for 20 minutes.

Heat the butter in a skillet. Add flour and cook gently for 2 minutes. Add milk and

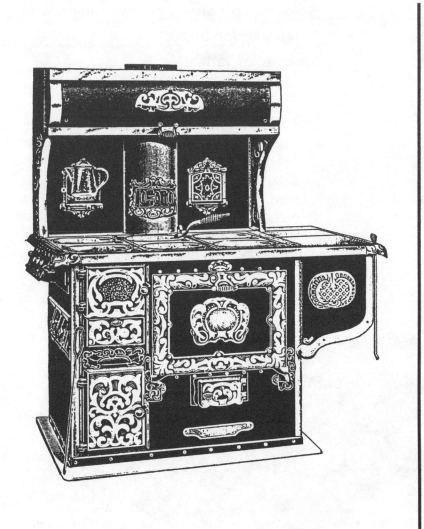

turmeric and cook until slightly thickened. Add to potato mixture.

Chop the nettles and add them to the soup with the chives. Simmer 5 minutes. Garnish with parsley and serve.

Four servings.

*If you can't find stinging nettle, you can use Chinese cabbage.

Low-Cal Fried Potatoes

If I tell you I'm eating potatoes for breakfast you'll say, "But why? Do you want to get fat as a butterball?" Well, the reason is, the refrigerator is full of potatoes and there is another crate in the basement. The farmers were selling them for six cents a pound.

My husband and I eat potatoes regularly. Potatoes are not a high calorie food. But you have to cook them so they taste good without piling on the butter, cream and oil. I love fried potatoes done in only ½ tablespoon of butter. It's possible.

My recipe preserves almost all the vitamin C. One medium-sized potato has twenty milligrams of vitamin C. (The recommended daily requirement of vitamin C according to the Department of Agriculture is forty-five milligrams.) You have to peel the potato and then instantly slice it into the skillet. Don't soak the potato in water. The flavor will end up in the water, so will the vitamin C.

3 medium potatoes, peeled and sliced

½ tablespoon butter

sprinkle of salt

Melt the butter in a heavy iron skillet. Place sliced potatoes in skillet and sprinkle lightly with salt. Cook over medium heat, turning from time to time so all slices are evenly browned. Do not cover.

The secret of these delicious potatoes is the innate flavor of the potatoes. Nothing is lost in the cooking and almost no calories are added.

Four servings.

I Don't Drive

I put it away again. The driving manual. That booklet you have to study in order to pass the driving test. Every once in a while I feel absolutely ashamed of myself for not having a driving license and I take out the driving manual and I say to everyone, "I'm going to get my license."

I know what you're saying by now. "You don't drive? How benighted can you be! Children of fourteen drive!" I know, and they drive very well.

I don't. I had a license once, for three years, in South America. All I had to do to get it was make right hand turns around the block. Nobody would ride with me. My friends said, "If it's your turn to drive we'll take a taxi."

My license ran out and I didn't renew it. Then we came back to the USA and everyone said, "You can't live here without driving a car." I know that and some day I'll get a license.

It's just that it's not very high on my list of priorities. We're a one-car family. Actually, we're a one-car, one-driver family and we seem to get along very well. We can walk almost everywhere we want to go. It's a mile to the university, two miles to the center of town, one and a half to the post office. Stores are everywhere, and besides, we don't buy that much. My husband was in Alaska last summer and I got along perfectly all right. The car sat in the garage. There's a bus system and I could ride, but generally I walk.

"Well," you'll say, "how about those hikes into the outdoors? Up mountains, across valleys? How do you get to the trails?" Right now we have carpools. Some people drive and the rest chip in money. That's not perfect because some people are using their cars more than others. I suppose eventually we might come to weekend tour buses or feeder buses. A bus would go to the end of the line in the morning and drop off the hikers with their knapsacks and come back at the end of the day and pick them up. Skiers do this all the time.

Still and all, I will get to work on this driving business. There are two good reasons. One is there could be an emergency and then I'll be sorry. Number two is I never have any identification with me. If you don't have a driver's license and you don't have credit cards, who are you? Do you even exist?

I think I'm waiting for a magic car. One that's very small, not noisy, and has no smell. Like an electric car. But even then do I need a whole mechanized contraption of two or three or four thousand pounds to get me from here to there? I guess it boils down to the fact that I have a bus mentality—or train or trolley. Leave the driving to someone else. If my feet won't take me, something going by will—and if it's not going by, why isn't it?

Hi-Pro Chili

This is my April Fool's recipe. I know the world is very serious. As Sean O'Casey said in his play *Juno and the Paycock,* (in which I once played Maisie Madigan): the world is in a ''state of chassis.'' The character using that expression meant chaos. I know the world is in a ''state of chassis'' but we still have to laugh once in a while.

I designed this recipe for an earthworm contest. I didn't win anything but I've had a lot of fun serving the chili. You could call it ''Chili Con Wormee.'' If ''chili con carne'' is chili with meat, then chili con wormee is—you guessed it—chili with nice little earthworms in it.

It really isn't so far out. Don't we eat oysters and mussels and snails? In South America I once ate a plate of baby eels. It's all good protein.

2 tablespoons oil

½ cup chopped onion

1 clove garlic, chopped

½ pound ground beef

½ cup prepared earthworms*

2 cups cooked kidney beans

2 cups chopped fresh tomato (or canned)

½ green pepper, chopped

1 teaspoon salt

½ teaspoon cumin

2 teaspoons chopped fresh oregano (or 1 teaspoon dried)

1 tablespoon chili powder

Saute the onion and garlic in the oil. Remove onions and garlic from oil, and add ground beef. Brown the meat.

Add all other ingredients and simmer, covered, over low heat for 1 hour. Serve with crackers, rice or tortillas.

Serves four.

*Wash the worms, then put them on a wet cornmeal diet for 2 days. Wash them again, then place them in a kettle with enough water to cover and boil for 3 minutes. Change the water and boil for 6 minutes. Dry on a paper towel. Place worms on a cookie sheet and bake in 350° oven until worms are crisp, about 10 minutes. Crumble into small bits.

Sprouted Wheat Pancakes with Creamed Smoked Salmon

Two and two make five when you sprout seeds and grains. You get more than the sum total of the vitamins and minerals there are in the seed or grain. That's because the seed is turning into a plant. Have you noticed the little green leaves on the alfalfa sprouts? Those leaves are reacting with sunlight in the process of photosynthesis. Vitamins A and C are being developed.

You can buy whole books on how to sprout. They are necessary because there are so many different kinds of seeds, grains, and legumes you can sprout. The different kinds take different methods and different lengths of time.

Wheat, for instance, can be sprouted in earth or in a jar. For this recipe I sprout the wheat in a jar and for only half the time called for to get proper wheat sprouts. Wheat sprouts done in a jar don't show green. You use them when the sprout is no longer than the length of the grain. That takes two days. Since I use them in twenty-four hours for the pancake recipe I don't expect to see any growth at all. But I know the new growth is beginning inside of the grain.

2 cups sprouted wheat (see method below)

2 cups low-fat milk

2 eggs, separated

2 teaspoons baking powder

½ teaspoon salt

2 tablespoons oil

For this recipe I sprout wheat only 24 hours. Wash the wheat, then soak it in water overnight. Drain and rinse. Place soaked wheat in sprouting jar or glass jar with cheesecloth fastened over opening. Rinse with warm water every 4 hours, except overnight. After 24 hours rinse and use. You will not see much evidence of sprouting but the wheat will be softened and perfect for this recipe.

Place 1 cup sprouted wheat and 1 cup milk in blender and blend until mixture thickens, about 3 minutes. Pour into a bowl. Repeat with the rest of the sprouted wheat and milk. Pour into bowl.

Beat the egg yolks and add with baking powder, salt and oil. Beat with fork or spoon until evenly mixed.

In a separate bowl beat the egg whites until stiff. Fold into wheat mixture. Bake on hot griddle.

Serve with Creamed Smoked Salmon.
Makes 16 - 20 pancakes.

How can I mention smoked salmon when we are being warned about carcinogens in the smoke? I believe that warning and I heed it. We smoke our fish very lightly; it is more of a smoke-cook process. And by the time we share with friends and neighbors, no one gets a huge amount.

It's amazing how much of life is a trade-off. In this recipe I'm trading off the sugar people usually put on pancakes in the form of heavy syrup. I don't like sweet syrup on pancakes. I like my pancakes savory, as my British friends in South America used to say. We'd be at a tea party and the host would ask, "Sweet or savory?" She meant, do you wish to start with a sandwich or something sweet.

My Hungarian mother was accustomed to pancakes (crepes) with cottage cheese or cabbage. We made a cream sauce to put on the pancakes, and in those Depression days we had only cabbage to add to the sauce. If we'd had smoked salmon we would have added it with delight.

I use kokanee salmon because that's the kind my husband catches and brings home. He has a smoker made out of a fifty-gallon oil drum and once or twice a year he smokes fish.

The recipe can be made with plain salmon, also with tuna.

Creamed Smoked Salmon

3 tablespoons butter

3 tablespoons flour

2 cups milk

1 cup skinned, deboned smoked salmon

Melt the butter in a skillet. Add flour and cook over low heat for 3 minutes, stirring constantly. Slowly add milk, stirring to avoid lumps. Cook and stir until sauce is thickened. Add salmon and mix gently. Serve hot.

Lamb's Quarter Quiche

I used to serve all my dinner guests pigweed. That's when I had forty packages of that edible wild green in my freezer. What a haul! I found a farmer's field full of it. That was a joy, but then my husband and I had to work until midnight, washing, blanching, cooling and packaging.

The kind of pigweed I had was lamb's quarter, *Chenopolium album*. Some people call it wild spinach. You can eat it raw or cooked, using any recipe you would use for spinach. The nutritive value is like that of spinach, high in vitamins A and C, with fair amounts of iron and potassium. I don't count on either spinach or lamb's quarter (or any member of that family) for my calcium even though the charts that list food values show a goodly amount of calcium in the plants. The chemical makeup of the spinach family includes high amounts of oxalic acid which combine with the calcium to make it unavailable to the body.

Lamb's Quarter Quiche is just as delicious as spinach quiche. You can make it with a whole wheat crust or a white flour crust.

2 tablespoons butter

3 tablespoons chopped onion

3 cups young lamb's quarter leaves, chopped (or use spinach)

3 large eggs, lightly beaten

1⅔ cups warm milk

½ teaspoon salt

dash of pepper

1 cup grated Swiss cheese

9-inch partially baked and cooled pie shell

dash of nutmeg

In a saucepan saute onion and lamb's quarter in butter for 5 minutes.

Beat eggs slightly in a mixing bowl, then add milk, salt and pepper and beat them together. Add the sauteed onion and lamb's quarter and mix.

Sprinkle cheese in the pie crust. Pour the egg mixture over cheese. Sprinkle with nutmeg.

Bake in preheated 325° oven 35 - 45 minutes, or until set. Let stand 10 minutes before serving.

Serves four.

Earth Journal

Earth Day is April 22. Do you remember the first Earth Day about ten years ago? School children planted trees, adults cleaned up rivers. Now it's time for another Earth Day. Here in Missoula we're having a whole week of Earth goings-on. My part is to take people on a wildflower walk.

I've got a new idea for the walk this year. I'm going to ask everybody to bring a notebook and label it Earth Journal. It's like a wildflower notebook or a birdwatcher's journal, but we're going to put everything in it. The flowers we see, the birds, maybe a coyote, or a muskrat. Maybe it'll be snowing and we'll put that in. It could snow on April 22.

The fun of keeping a nature journal is that you can look back at last year's entries and you know what to expect. You call up a friend and say, "Let's go see if the trillium is in bloom," or the yellow violets, or the blue bells. Your friend will say, "It's too early."

"Aha," you'll say, "I have it in my notebook that last year on April 15th I saw a yellow violet, a blue violet, and a dogtooth violet," (which is really a lily and not a violet at all).

You also need to write down where you saw the flower. You need the date and the place so you know when and where to go to find it again the next year.

We used to pick flowers and bring them home, but that was in the old days when there were fewer people and more flowers. My neighbors tell me they used to pick bouquets of larkspur and lupine right where our houses are now. That's the way it is. So we don't pick wildflowers any more. We take our notebook and we write in it, "First blue phlox — April 5th, 1980. First yellow bell — April 15th."

I put garden flowers in my notebook too. I like to know when the first crocus opens, the first daffodil, the first tulip. It doesn't have to be in my garden. The whole city of Missoula is my garden. The Clark Fork River too, and Waterworks Hill. It's all my garden.

That's the reason for my nature walk on Earth Day. I want everyone to feel that the Earth is our garden. The flowers, the trees, the coyote, the muskrat, the river, the mountains — they belong to all of us.

The notebook will help us remember. What we write down this year will be like an old friend next year. "Hello daffodil," you'll say. "Last year you bloomed in March, this year you're starting in April. Well, it was a hard winter. Next year it'll be better. So long."

I started keeping a wildflower notebook back in grade school. The teacher put a gold star on the blackboard for the person who first smelled the arbutus. We didn't pick arbutus even then. It was already rare. But I can smell it right now.

There'll be children on my wildflower hike, and college students, and business people, and senior citizens. We'll walk in rain or shine, we'll write in our notebooks, and then we'll come home and join the Street Fair. That's part of Earth Day too.

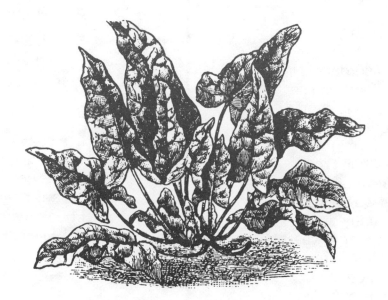

Seaweed Ratatouille

How could he do it? This dinner guest picked out every piece of seaweed from his stew and piled it on his bread plate.

"What are you doing, Bill?" I scolded. Bill was an old friend and was accustomed to being gently chided by me.

"I don't know what this is but it won't sell," Bill answered. He was referring to the old joke about the drunk who bet he could name any drink the bartender could mix, but the bartender finally passed him a glass of plain water. "I don't know what this is," the drunk said, "but it won't sell."

We won't pay any attention to Bill. He is an international traveler and believes the only way to stay clear of intestinal disorders is to live on steak, french fries and good whiskey.

I go along with the theory that one should eat many different kinds of food. One never knows what undiscovered magic might be in a new food. I'm always amazed when I read that oldtime Indians actually ate more different species of plants that we do today. They collected seeds from so many grasses, for instance. We might spend a whole week eating nothing but wheat, orange juice, meat, eggs, milk, peas, corn and potatoes.

Of course I also have to admit I was just having fun with Bill. I knew he wouldn't eat seaweed.

1 large onion, thinly sliced

1 clove garlic, minced

4 tablespoons oil

⅔ cup seaweed (dulse), washed, soaked and cooked

1 small sweet red pepper, sliced

2 cups diced eggplant

2 large tomatoes, diced

1 cup corn

pinch of paprika

½ tablespoon chopped fresh basil (or ½ teaspoon dried)

½ teaspoon dried oregano

In a heavy saucepan saute the onion and garlic in oil. Add all the other ingredients. Simmer, covered, for 30 minutes, or until the eggplant is tender.

Four servings.

In Chile this dish was served with parsleyed potatoes. Rice would be fine, or thick slices of whole wheat bread. Other types of seaweed besides dulse can be used. In Chile I used sea lettuce.

Easy Oatmeal Bread

Thanks to Lillian Klawitter, Missoula.

1 cup regular oatmeal

2 cups boiling water

1½ tablespoons dry yeast

⅓ cup lukewarm water

¼ cup honey or molasses

¼ cup vegetable oil

½ cup powdered milk

6 cups whole wheat flour

2 teaspoons salt

Combine oatmeal and boiling water. Let cool for 20 minutes.

Sprinkle yeast over lukewarm water. Let rest 5 minutes. Stir and add to oatmeal mixture. Add honey, oil and powdered milk and stir well.

Combine flour and salt and add to oatmeal mixture. Stir with wooden spoon, then knead 5 minutes. Add a bit more flour if the dough is very sticky.

Place dough in an oiled bowl and let it rest in a warm, draft-free place until it doubles in bulk. Knead again. Shape dough into two regular or round loaves and place them in greased pans. Let rise 10 minutes.

Bake in preheated 325° oven for 45-50 minutes.

Sourdough Bread

Can you imagine a graduate student having time to make sourdough bread? John Pierce of the University of Montana makes sourdough bread as casually as your mother makes meat loaf on Thursdays. It's John's staple bread. He varies it by adding anything he finds around the kitchen. It might be cottage cheese, sour cream, sprouted wheat.

Once in a while John makes sourdough bagels. It's the same dough as for bread but of course you have to shape the bagels, boil them in salted water and then bake them. Bagels are a treat; bread is a staple.

John's sourdough starter did not come from a sourdough miner in Alaska. I know some people who actually have that kind of starter. John's is only eight years old and he started it himself from a package of yeast.

You can have lots of fun with sourdough. You can carry a jar of the starter with you when you go backpacking and make bread, muffins and pancakes along the trail.

Actually, pancakes are a must if you are a sourdough owner because sourdough starter should be used at least once a week to keep it in prime condition.

6½ cups whole wheat flour

3 cups milk

½ cup cold water

½ cup dry bulgur wheat or raw oatmeal

¾ cup sourdough starter

4 eggs

2 teaspoons salt

½ cup honey

¼ cup oil

1 teaspoon cinnamon (optional)

3 cups unbleached white flour (more or less)

This is a two-day operation. On the evening of the first day, put 3½ cups whole wheat flour into a large mixing bowl. Scald milk, then pour it on flour. Rinse out milk pan with ½ cup cold water and add that to flour-milk mixture. Add bulgur or oatmeal. Mix. Let cool to lukewarm.

Add starter. Mix in thoroughly. Cover bowl

with cookie sheet and leave on kitchen counter. The mixture will start bubbling even at 50° temperature. Stir once in a while. Let stand 24 hours.

On the evening of the second day, add eggs, salt, honey, oil and cinnamon. Mix. Add 3 cups whole wheat flour. Mix. Empty dough on floured board and start kneading, adding white flour cup by cup. Knead until dough is no longer sticky. You'll be adding about 3 cups of flour.

Place dough in greased bowl and let rise in warm place until doubled, about 1 ½ hours. Punch down and divide into 3 or 4 loaves, depending on size of your breadpans. Place loaves in greased pans. Let rise until double in size, about 30 minutes. Bake in preheated 350° oven 45 minutes.

If you want freshly baked bread for breakfast, place the unbaked loaves, after they have risen for 30 minutes, in the refrigerator. The next morning remove from refrigerator, place in preheated 350° oven and bake 45 minutes.

Thanks to John Pierce, Missoula, Montana

Good Health

If I say to you that I can run a mile, you'll say, "That's nothing. Anybody can do that." But I'm fifty-nine years old and I spent a lot of years not doing anything. So I'm pretty happy about it.

The next point is: what's so hot about being able to run a mile? Well, I think if you're happy with the shape you're in, fine. But I wasn't happy with the shape I was in. I'm still the same five pounds overweight. I weigh one hundred twenty-six pounds and I'm only five feet three. According to the charts I should be one hundred and ten, but I think one hundred twenty would be fine for me. So I'm still five or six pounds more than I want to be. But that's not what I mean by the shape I'm in. I mean I can do a lot more than I could five years ago.

I can run over to the university — that's a mile. Then I can swim and walk back, do whatever I have to around the house, and then if I have an evening class I can walk over to the university again, give my class or go to a lecture, and walk home again.

And I haven't had a cold in three years. That's what I mean by being in good shape. Not the kind of shape a model has. Now why should I care about this shape or state of health I'm in? Every day we hear about a new pollution, a new additive, a new preservative that has been doing us wrong. And how about all the ones that no one has found out about? And can you get away from them? They're in the air, in the water, in your soup, in your vegetables, in your fruit, eggs, milk.

So what can you do? I figure the better shape you're in the better off you are. And you have to do it yourself. Doctors and hospitals are all over the place but in the long run you've got to do it yourself.

So I say the best thing I can do for myself is to put myself into as good shape as I can. First, so I can stay away from medicine and doctors, hospitals, drugstores. And secondly, so I can resist all these odd substances we have around us.

There are people who can be right in the middle of typhoid and they don't get typhoid. There are people who work with poisonous chemicals and it's as if they were immune. So, if we can't hope to get rid of all the odd substances we have in, on and around us, we have to say to our body, "Be strong."

I was eating Flathead cherries last summer. I knew they'd been sprayed seven times. Maybe the rain washed the spray off and maybe it didn't. So I said to myself, "Cells of my body, gird up your loins. Because I'm going to feast on these cherries and who knows what all has been done to them!"

If you are a student of eastern philosophy you might say I'm revving up my yin and yang or my electric field. Whatever way you want to look at it, it comes to this: you've got to give your body all the help you can — with exercise, with food that has been the least tampered with. And don't forget your spirit. You have to rev up your spirit to do battle.

Rhubarb Pie with Dandelion Flower Topping

I don't eat many desserts and I don't like to advocate them, but there are certain occasions that would not be complete without a dessert.

A rhubarb pie is a celebration of spring. We have watched the pink crowns poking through the ground, we have watched the first leaves uncurl, we have waited for the petioles (the leaf stalks) to become thick and hefty. A rhubarb pie is the end result of our watching and waiting.

My one rhubarb pie of the season, like my huckleberry pie on the 4th of July, a pumpkin pie for Thanksgiving, and a mince pie for Christmas, is necessary for me. It's a tradition. It's ritual.

I think where we went wrong with our eating habits is when we made sweets an everyday thing. I grew up in the days when a family baked once a week and stores were five miles away by horse and buggy. A dessert was something you had after Sunday dinner.

I know people don't live like that today. We are surrounded by sweets twenty-four hours a day. They are in your cupboard, in your freezer, in every store on every street corner, and in machines in the schools. To avoid sugar we'd have to be like that religious sect called the Essenes, who ate nothing prepared by any hands but theirs. But we can cut down. A sweet is a treat and it should be reserved for special occasions.

The dandelion flower topping is for fun. One has to have fun with cooking. The idea came from Ilze Mueller in St. Paul, Minnesota. She wrote to me about a recipe I once aired on National Public Radio. I was adding dandelion flowers to pancake batter. Ilze Mueller wrote to me and said she got so enthused she not only tried the pancakes but she tried the same idea with a rhubarb pie. Her letter said the pie was a great success. "I and my friends felt like discoverers," she wrote.

*Since I bake very few pies I am not going to advocate one or another recipe for the crust. I would never win a prize for my pie crust. You go ahead and use your own recipe. I hope it's whole wheat.

Adapted from a recipe sent by Ilze Mueller of St. Paul, Minnesota

**pie dough for 9-inch crust and
    lattice-work top***

3½ cups diced rhubarb

1 cup sugar

pinch of cinnamon

1 egg

½ cup light cream

2 tablespoons flour

**petals from 50 dandelion flowers,
    all green parts removed**

Roll out dough and fit into a 9-inch pie pan. Save the leftover dough for a lattice-work top.

Place the rhubarb in a bowl. Sprinkle with ½ cup sugar mixed with cinnamon.

Beat the egg, and add cream, ½ cup sugar, flour and dandelion petals. Mix in with rhubarb and pour all into pie pan. Top with strips of dough woven into lattice-work.

Bake in preheated 400° oven for 10 minutes. Reduce the heat to 325° and bake about 45 minutes.

Summer is a Salad Bar

Mel's Lunch Salad

I think the salad bar is the innovation of the century. If America discovered it or started it, good for us. For decades nutritionists have been telling us, "Eat more raw food," and now, finally, even traditional steak and chop restaurants display a salad bar. A vegetarian can dine out with a meat-and-potatoes type without either person feeling thwarted.

A salad bar can be a home fixture too. You can use it as lunch, a major part of dinner, an after-school snack, or for T.V. munchies. The salad bar can be as simple as one platter of cut up raw vegetables, or it can have both raw and cooked vegetables, a plate of fruit and prepared salads.

Carrot and celery sticks, cherry tomatoes, broccoli, cauliflower and strips of bell pepper are basic, but really you can put almost anything in your display: raw spinach, raw peas, green onions, cucumber slices, zucchini, turnip, Jerusalem artichoke, watercress. The dips or dressings can be both low-calorie and nutritious: hummus, tofu, cottage cheese, yogurt. The breads or crackers served can be one hundred percent whole grain. People are learning to bake, and to eat, whole grain products. I'm always amazed when I visit the thrift shop outlet of the local bread factory and find people snatching up the honey whole wheat bread like a prize. People stand in line waiting for the door to open so they can snatch the whole wheat bread!

My husband would be aghast if you called him a health food person, but this is his typical lunch:

a huge raw salad

one slice of stoneground whole wheat bread with old-fashioned peanut butter and honey

a saucedish of homemade yogurt with homemade applesauce or canned plums

a hot drink made of powdered milk and blackstrap molasses

Now I'm not saying that Mel does not eat hamburgers and milk shakes. He does at times, but most of the time Mel and I eat plain good food. On days when Mel feels fat he eats the salad with no dressing at all. On days he feels thin he adds half of an avocado.

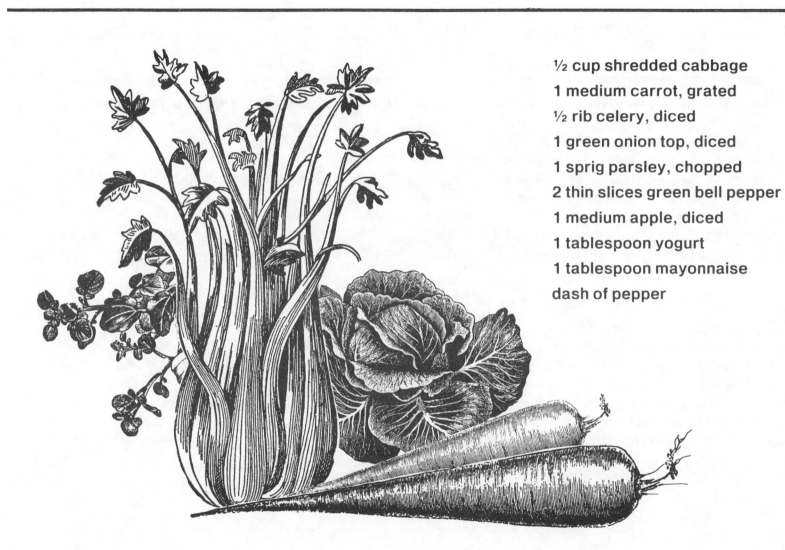

½ cup shredded cabbage

1 medium carrot, grated

½ rib celery, diced

1 green onion top, diced

1 sprig parsley, chopped

2 thin slices green bell pepper

1 medium apple, diced

1 tablespoon yogurt

1 tablespoon mayonnaise

dash of pepper

Note To A Mouse

"Are you writing notes to mice?" my husband asked.

"What do you mean?" I said.

"Well," my husband said, "I come home from a trip and I find a letter on the garage floor, a letter written by you and addressed to the mouse that ate your crackers."

I had to laugh. "Was it a mouse?" I said. "Are you sure?"

"I'm going to set a trap and I'll show you," my husband said.

Then we both laughed. I was positive it was a burglar. So I wrote him a note. (Now you see I'm discriminating. How do I know the burglar was a he?) Anyway, I wrote the burglar a note: "I don't mind your eating my crackers," I said, "but please don't take my poor little garden tools and the lawn furniture. Thank you." And I signed my name.

Actually, we wouldn't have lost much if a burglar took everything in the garage. Or in the house, for that matter. I've always operated on the principle that burglars have already been in our house. They've been in, looked around, and decided there was nothing worth their time so they left.

Everything we own is secondhand, so if our things were stolen we'd just go to a few rummage sales or secondhand stores and restock.

It's a blessing in a way. I remember years ago when my husband and I were transferred to South America by his company. We went by ship. Our luggage was broken into on the dock in Valparaiso. That's what the insurance company said, anyway. It didn't happen on the ship so they refused to pay for it. We probably didn't have the right kind of insurance. We were young and dumb.

It was my belongings that were taken. My new two-piece bathing suit, my class ring, my pearls—in those days women wore pearls. Mine were imitation. I was devastated. I lost five pounds over that robbery, and over the fact that the insurance company weaseled out of paying. I should have gone right down to the company's office, sat on the floor, and said, "I will not move from here." I would have had to say it in Spanish: *Voy a plantarme aquí hasta el fin del mundo*. That translates into "I'm going to plant myself right here until the end of the world."

Of course I was too shy to do anything like that. I was a proper young thing so all I did was cry—over my class ring, my brand new imitation pearls, my brand new two-piece bathing suit.

Slowly I filled up a big house in Chile with things. We lived there for eighteen years. Then we were moved back to the United States. We sold or gave away everything. We came back with the same two suitcases we went down with.

That broke the spell of things. Things are only things, whether they are nice things or secondhand things or rummage sale things. I don't ever want to worry about things again. If a burglar wants to come into the garage, fine. Take that secondhand lawnmower that we bought for three dollars because the owner wanted a gasoline mower. Take that spading fork with one tine missing. Take the ice chest that I picked up alongside Highway I-90. Take the lawn furniture that came from alleys.

If I feel that way why did I write a note to the burglar? Why did I say "I don't mind your eating my crackers, but please don't take my poor little things"? Well, you have to let a burglar know you are aware of his/her presence. Besides, to replace everything in the garage would take me a year of rummage sales.

So I'm glad it was a mouse that ate the crackers, even though they were very good crackers, homemade whole wheat with peanut oil.

That's a well-fed mouse.

Breakfast Salad

I am a chewer rather than a drinker so I have never been content with drinking fruit juice, drinking milk, etc. for a meal. I like to sit and move my jaws. It's relaxing.

There is plenty of protein in this breakfast salad. If you are on a non-salt or low-salt diet you can omit the cottage cheese, which is really very salty (I'd like to see cottage cheese made with less salt) and use a low-salt cheese or tofu.

The avocado and the alfalfa sprouts are the raw ingredients. I like to eat something raw with each meal.

½ avocado, peeled

½ apricot, fresh or canned

¼ cup alfalfa sprouts

¼ cup cooked garbanzo beans

2 tablespoons yogurt

1 tablespoon cashew nut pieces

Mound cottage cheese on avocado half. Top with apricot half. Place sprouts and garbanzos around center mound. Add the yogurt and cashew nut pieces last.

Serves one.

Corn-Stuffed Tomato

This is a delight not only for the stomach, but also for the eyes. It's that pretty.

In South America we varied the recipe by sometimes omitting the basil and adding fresh coriander (cilantro) leaves. If you find cilantro in the market try it. It looks a bit like parsley but the taste is very distinctive.

4 large tomatoes

2 cups cooked corn

¼ cup diced green pepper

3 tablespoons finely chopped onion

½ tablespoon chopped fresh basil (or ½ teaspoon dried)

pinch of black pepper

1 tablespoon chopped parsley

4 tablespoons mayonnaise

4 sprigs parsley for decoration

Cut a thin slice from the bottom of each tomato so it will sit on the plate. Cut a slice from the stem end and scoop out the pulp. Let the pulp drain in a colander (save the liquid for soup). Dice the pulp and mix with corn, green pepper, onion, basil, black pepper, chopped parsley and mayonnaise.

Fill the tomatoes with the mixture and place a sprig of parsley on top of each one. Set on a bed of lettuce.

Four servings.

Savory Four-Bean Salad

This is not a sweet four-bean salad. That's why I call it Savory Four-Bean Salad. I see no reason why we should stick to the old American beans-with-sugar idea. Baked beans are like a dessert—they are that sweet! My Hungarian tradition (and my South American sojourn) have left me with a complete antipathy to sugar in beans.

I will admit that cooking beans without piling on the sugar is a little more work. Most of us are not adept at using herbs. As a matter of fact, we're not adept at cooking beans, period. How often do we hear people say, ''I made beans but no one liked them. And we all had gas.''

I throw away the soaking water from the beans, and also the first cooking water, removed after half an hour of cooking. Yes, I'm losing some of the nutritive value but it's a tradeoff for less gas in the stomach.

There are two ways to cook beans. One is to soak them overnight and the next day proceed with the cooking. The other is for same-day eating: Bring the beans to boil in cold water and let them boil for two minutes. Remove them from the heat, cover and let stand one hour.

With either method I drain off that soaking water, add fresh water, cook, covered, for one half hour, then drain again. Then I add fresh water and cook the beans until they are tender. This is the final cooking and the liquid stays with the beans.

Try different types of beans. I like pinto beans, black beans, lima beans, garbanzo beans. Navy beans are not my favorite. You can try marinating beans in vinegar, oil and herb dressings, without sugar.

Bake beans with herbs. Or with apple. (I put a recipe for baked beans with apple in the winter section.)

1 cup pinto beans, cooked and drained

1 cup red kidney beans, cooked
and drained

1 cup garbanzo beans, cooked and drained

1 cup green beans, lightly steamed and
cut into 1-inch pieces

1 cup diced celery

2 tablespoons chopped onion

2 tablespoons chopped green bell pepper

¼ teaspoon paprika

¼ teaspoon mustard powder

1 tablespoon lemon juice

3 tablespoons cider vinegar

½ cup oil

1 tablespoon chopped chives

1 tablespoon chopped parsley

Mix all the ingredients except chives and parsley. Let it sit in the refrigerator overnight. Sprinkle chives and parsley on top just before serving.

After making this basic recipe two or three times, try adding oregano, thyme or basil.

Serves four.

Chewing Snoose At Eighty-Three

"You chewed snuff? I said to Eunice. "Copenhagen snuff? Snoose?" That's what they call snuff. Snoose. I was talking to my eighty-three-year-old friend Eunice. At midnight. Yes, at midnight. She had just come home from an antique auction. She does that on the side—buys and sells antiques. At eighty-three years old.

Here she was in my kitchen in her long dress. "When I go to an antique sale," she said to me, "I dress like an antique." At eighty-three you might think Eunice is on her way to being an antique. Not at all. Eunice has more energy than two people half her age. In fact, one night not long ago she stayed up all night getting ready for an antique sale and then went to the sale.

"What's your secret?" I said to her one day.

"I don't know," she said. "I've got too much to do to think about it."

That's her secret, of course. She's got a lot of things to do. At eighty-three she has things to do that she loves doing. She was square dancing until a couple of years ago. And she goes out. She has a little white car, and she flies in and out in that little car every single day. Once I asked her to talk on the radio, and guess who took whom to the radio station. She drove me in her car, and she's eighty-three and I'm fifty-nine.

When I go huckleberrying and I take her a quart of berries, do you know what arrives at my house the next day? Four huckleberry muffins hot from the oven. "Eat one right now, Kim," she says, "while it's hot. There's one for your husband and two in case company comes."

Company is very important to Eunice. Friends, relatives, all kinds of company. Maybe that's why she's never lonesome. She has friends, family, church people, and students from the school she used to teach in. On her eighty-second birthday she received eighty-two birthday cards.

Does Eunice eat or drink anything special? No. She eats an apple a day, some meat or fish or chicken and lots of vegetables. She loves vegetables. Not much dessert—hardly any. She drinks a little wine, even some whiskey. Does she smoke? No. Then why the snuff? That goes to show Eunice is young in heart. She'll try things. She was at this antique show and the man at the next table kept putting snuff in his mouth. (Eunice was telling me about this at midnight sitting in my kitchen.)

"This man," she said, "seemed to be enjoying tremendously this wad of tobacco under his tongue, or wherever he was putting it." So Eunice asked him what it was like.

"Do you smoke?" he asked.

"No," Eunice said.

"Well, then you wouldn't like it," he said. "But would you like to try it?"

"Yes," Eunice said. So he passed over his little round box, and Eunice took a pinch and put it in her mouth.

"How do you like it?" the man asked.

"I don't," Eunice said.

"Well, spit it out then," the man said.

"Oh, I chewed it up and swallowed it," Eunice said.

"Oh my," the man said, "I hope you don't get sick."

Eunice didn't get sick at all. She finished the day at the antique show, went out to dinner in her long dress and earrings, came home at midnight, saw my light on and came over to chat.

Eunice, I wouldn't mind being like you at eighty-three. I might even try some snuff. But I'll keep it under my tongue. I won't swallow it.

Sweet Potato Salad

I first tasted sweet potato salad not at a salad bar but at a picnic. I especially remember it because—well, of course because it was the first time I tasted sweet potato salad, but also because it was the kind of picnic I heartily approve of. Nobody had to work all night; we didn't bring iceboxes and refrigerators; we didn't even build a fire. Somebody called somebody and said, "Let's go on a picnic. Just bring what you can throw into a basket in two minutes."

This was not a *dejeuner sur l'herbe* with roast capon and chilled white wine. There was no babbling brook or mountain lake. This was a picnic of leftovers at an old reservoir.

But we had a splendid day. No fuss, no muss, we had time to enjoy, we had the energy to walk. The reservoir was surrounded by green meadows. It had yellow iris at one end. And we crossed a stile. How often in life does a person cross a stile? You know what a stile is? It's what the old woman in the nursery rhyme tried to get her pig to cross. The pig wouldn't cross and the old woman couldn't get to market.

We crossed the stile (little steps up and down) and we spread out our leftovers in a green meadow. We listened to a meadowlark, watched butterflies, identified flowers and I delved into recipes for sweet potato salad. Marvelous for picnics, we agreed: no mayonnaise—no refrigeration necessary.

2 cups diced cooked sweet potatoes

1½ cups diced celery

½ cup diced sweet red pepper

¼ teaspoon salt

½ cup chopped almonds

½ cup sprouted sunflower seeds*

1 cup yogurt

1 tablespoon chopped parsley

Mix all ingredients except parsley. Sprinkle the parsley on top just before serving. Serves four.

*Sunflower seeds for this recipe should be sprouted only to ¼ inch. If you don't have sprouts ready you can substitute lightly toasted sunflower seeds.

54

Dilled Yogurt Dressing

Do you have friends who are Ketchup-on-Everything types? Mel and I knew a family like that in South America. They were American, sent down by the Air Force. They had to import ketchup by the case and even then they ran out. I might have gone that same route if Mel and I'd had import privileges. As it was, I followed South American cooks around, asking "What's this? What's that?"

One of the great things I learned was about herbs: what they were, how they tasted, how they were used. I followed my housekeeper (my friend, my confidante) to the open-air market to find out all I could about this new and mysterious food category. I took the bus to the large central market to the herb shops where I bought dried herbs by the gram (South America uses the gram and kilo weight system). I learned cumin, coriander, turmeric, basil, anise, tarragon, saffron—oh, what smells! What delight!

I'm glad to report that right here in the U.S. more and more people are cooking with herbs. It's a marvelous way to cut down on sugar and salt and still have flavor.

Dill is a flavor associated with dill pickles but we can use this herb in many other ways.

It goes with fish, cucumbers in sour cream or yogurt, potato salad made without sweet pickle relish, cottage cheese, salad dressings. Dill can be used fresh (grow it in your garden) or dried. The feathery foliage is often called dill weed.

½ **cup low-fat yogurt**

2 **tablespoons mayonnaise**

½ **tablespoon snipped dill weed**

1 **teaspoon grated onion**

1 **teaspoon minced chives**

¼ **cup cottage cheese (optional)**

Mix all ingredients.

This makes a little more than ½ cup of dressing. Stored in a closed jar, it will keep one week in the refrigerator.

Tofu Dip

Tofu, which is soybean cheese, is inexpensive, high in protein and easily digested. It has no taste really, so you have to add the taste. Since tofu is low in calories you can add mayonnaise without loading the calorie count.

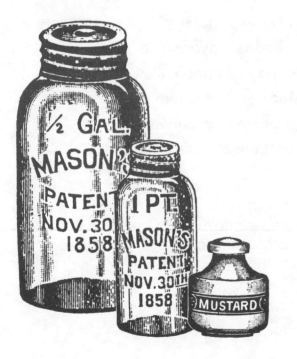

¼ **pound tofu**

3 tablespoons mayonnaise

½ **teaspoon prepared mustard**

1 teaspoon lemon juice

1 teaspoon minced chives

1 teaspoon chopped parsley

dash of salt

Mash the tofu with a fork. Mix in the other ingredients. For the best taste, make the night before you plan to use it. This will keep in a closed jar, refrigerated, for up to one week.

Makes one half cup.

Hummus

Hummus is a new taste for many people. We aren't accustomed to garbanzo beans (also called chick peas) mashed up with sesame seed paste and garlic. That's what hummus is.

Sesame seed paste is called tahini and though it looks rather like peanut butter, the taste is quite exotic.

Hummus can be a spread for sandwiches or a dip for raw vegetables.

2 cups cooked garbanzo beans (reserve the cooking water)

3 cloves garlic, mashed

½ teaspoon salt

½ cup tahini

juice of ½ lemon

¼ cup bean liquid (more if necessary for proper consistency)

3 tablespoons chopped parsley

dash of cayenne pepper

Mash the garbanzo beans with a fork or grind them in a meat grinder. In a separate bowl mash the garlic, then mix in the salt and tahini. Add lemon juice and a tablespoon at a time of the bean liquid, beating after each spoonful of liquid until smooth and creamy.

Add tahini mixture a little at a time to garbanzo bean puree, again beating until smooth and creamy. Mix in chopped parsley and cayenne pepper.

Makes about two and one half cups.

The Sacred Home Of The Grizzly Bear

"This is the home of the grizzly bear." I said that as we were driving into Glacier Park. The snow was deep on the mountains, so we couldn't go through the park. Going-to-the-Sun Highway was closed.

But I could look into the park and see the tall blue mountains piled with snow. We stood and looked up at those cold awesome mountains. This is the home of the grizzlies. The bears have gone into their dens for the winter to hibernate. Some of the mother bears will give birth while in their dens under the snow.

As I stood, the snow swirled around me, and cold air rolled down from the majestic peaks.

Suddenly I thought, "This is the home of the gods." I didn't mean the gods of Olympus. I didn't mean anything literally. But somehow I got the feeling we could leave this place alone; leave it without tracks, so to speak, without trails. We could hike in other places and backpack in other wildernesses. We could leave the mountains in Glacier to the grizzly bear—to the spirit of the grizzly bear, if we want to put it that way.

My husband and I are backpackers. We love to go where there is no one, but we don't need to go to the innermost mountains of Glacier Park. We could settle for a bus going through on the Going-to-the-Sun Highway. We could stop at Logan Pass and look down and up and think about the grizzly bear roaming tall and silver in the heart of the mountains. That's enough. We don't have to meet him face to face. We can bring our children and say to them as we stand on Logan Pass (and no farther): "That's the home of the grizzly bear. That's a mysterious place."

Vegetable Melange in Peanut Butter Sauce

Now that the hot vegetable salad has been invented and we are using the stir-fry method for whole meals, we can combine the idea of a hot meal with the modern no-loss-in-nutrients style of cooking.

I was making a carrot and celery stir-fry dish one day when I suddenly had a hankering for the taste of peanut butter. I spooned out a dollop of peanut butter and instead of eating it or putting it on bread, I stirred it into my carrots and celery. I tasted the mixture gingerly but Hallelujah! it was delicious. Then I remembered that a neighbor of mine had once served me a very exotic dish—I think it was from some part of the Far East—that had a peanut butter sauce. So I'm not being that different. You can try this dish and know it has an authentic base somewhere in the world.

1 teaspoon oil

1 cup carrots, sliver-cut

1 cup onion, cut in thin wedges

1 cup celery, sliced diagonally

1 cup sugar snap peas (pods, really)

¼ cup green bell pepper, diced

3 tablespoons dried milk

⅓ cup old-fashioned peanut butter

½ cup vegetable stock or water

¼ cup bean sprouts

2 tablespoons minced parsley

Heat oil in heavy skillet. Add carrots, onion, celery, snap peas and bell pepper. Saute 5 minutes. Turn off heat. Cover skillet and let stand.

In separate pan add dried milk and peanut butter to vegetable stock or water. Heat until ingredients blend into creamy sauce. Stir sauce into hot vegetables. Add bean sprouts.

Return to heat, cover and steam 5 minutes, or until vegetables are just tender. Add parsley. Serve on hot steamed brown rice.

Serves four.

Porotos Granados

We called this dish *Porotos Granados* in Chile, but the other day I ran across an article about the Iroquois Indians and it talked about the "Indian trinity of plants"—corn, beans and squash, which are the ingredients of *Porotos Granados.* How could the Indians in Chile and the Iroquois in New York have the same dish? But there you are—corn, beans and squash.

When I ate *Porotos Granados* in Chile I didn't know they were the "Indian trinity of plants" but I did know that Lucy my housekeeper always came home from the *feria* (outdoor market) with all three. From midsummer to frost she came home with a kilo of beans (pods and all, like unshelled lima beans), a chunk of winter squash and two ears of corn.

She cut the corn off the cob, uncooked. The milk would splatter all over and Lucy's face would be dotted with white. We would laugh. Then I'd help her shell the beans. We would sit together under the walnut tree, chattering like magpies. Lucy loved to talk and she had to have an audience.

We peeled the squash, cut it up, then cooked all three vegetables together in a little water. The squash disintegrated, providing the corn and beans with a lovely yellow-orange sauce. Flavored with salt, pepper and butter, *Porotos Granados* was a dish fit for company.

It was better than our American succotash, much better. Well, there was that marvelous Chilean pumpkin-squash, a variety rather like Hubbard but creamier when cooked. Then the beans were a special buttery type, so special the plants produced very little and were very susceptible to disease. The beans always had spots on them and some had to be thrown away. No big agriculturist would grow them for market. Even in the small farmers' markets they became scarce as new kinds of beans were introduced. We got more for our money with the newer beans, but not one had the taste of the old *Coscorone.* Give up something to gain something.

1 medium-sized onion, diced

2 tablespoons butter

1 cup cooked fresh lima beans

1 cup fresh sweet corn, scraped
    off the ears raw*

1 cup winter squash, raw, diced

1 teaspoon chopped fresh basil

½ teaspoon salt

dash of paprika

½ cup milk or vegetable broth

In a heavy saucepan, fry the onion in butter. Add all other ingredients. Simmer, covered, until squash is tender and mixture is creamy-thick. If it's too thick add more liquid. Serves four.

*To scrape corn from cobs, make a cut with a sharp knife down the middle of each row of kernels. Cut tips off of kernels, and with dull edge of the knife, scrape the cob clean.

Taste Brings Back Memories

"Why are you eating those scrawny little peaches?" my friend Terry said to me. We were walking in a friend's orchard and I was picking peaches from a tiny bent-over tree.

"I don't know why," I said. It's something I'm trying to remember. Have you ever eaten something and suddenly you're somewhere else? The taste takes you to another time and place? I know smells can do that, and sounds — music for instance, or a bell or a whistle. But I didn't know a taste could do it until I was standing in this old orchard eating a scrawny peach from a tiny misshapen tree that was going back to its primeval ancestor.

The peach wasn't good. It was small, the pit was large, the skin was fuzzy, the flesh was mealy instead of juicy. It was a terrible peach but as I ate it I got a warm feeling. But why?

I ate another one and another one while I examined the feeling. Suddenly it came to me. It wasn't the taste. It was the memory. I was back in my childhood visiting the Bushwhackers.

Oh, it was terrible that we used that name. These were people and I loved visiting them. But we did call them Bushwhackers. Well, people called us names too. We were Hunkies or Krautheads. My father and mother came from Budapest. So we were Hunkies and these people who lived back in the hills were Bushwhackers.

They wove baskets for a living. It was during the Depression. Today we would call these people artists and we would sell the baskets in an art fair for a good price. They were real baskets made from willow splints.

I'm trying to think why I liked visiting these families so much. Was it because they gave me dime detective magazines to read? Or was it the huge project of going for the visit? It took all day and we always got home after dark. I never went alone. One of my little sisters always went with me.

What an expedition! A long winding road through old abandoned farms, old orchards, past old houses that were half falling down and had fifteen layers of wallpaper, one on top of another.

It was a little scary, especially coming home. It would be getting dark and the tree frogs — we called them

peepers — would start peeping. That's a very scary sound.

But we always stopped to eat peaches. The trees were in a corner of the orchard near an old house. Nobody watered those trees, nobody pruned them. The peaches were small and not at all juicy. But they were warm from the sun and the taste was mixed with the feeling that we were in an adventure. Suppose somebody came out of that old house and said, "Hey, what are you doing here?" Anything could happen, especially with those dime detectives under my arm. They were atrocious magazines!

All this I'm tasting when I eat these small scrawny peaches from this tree so far away from the Hudson Valley in New York State, but the same mealy inside and the same fuzzy outside and warm from the sun. Who was it said we live on other things besides bread and butter? Oh, we need small wild peaches and small wild cherries and small wild plums. I wish I had one of those small wild baskets to put everything in. I'd never call anyone a Bushwhacker again.

Hungarian Pumpkin

I remember this from my childhood. My mother cooked it in summer, while the pumpkins were small, green and new. The idea here is to braise the vegetable—which means to cook in a little water but not to throw the water away. My Hungarian mother never threw the cooking water away.

You can use this same recipe for any kind of squash—summer, winter or zucchini. The summer squash and zucchini would require less cooking time, perhaps only five or ten minutes.

½ cup chopped onion

3 tablespoons butter

3 cups young, immature pumpkin (still green), peeled and cut in small cubes

2 tablespoons water

½ teaspoon salt

½ teaspoon paprika

1 tablespoon chopped parsley

1 cup sour cream or yogurt

Saute the onion in the butter. Add pumpkin, water and salt. Cover the pot and simmer for 20 minutes, or until pumpkin is tender but not mushy. Turn off the heat and add remaining ingredients, stirring gently. Serve at once.

If it is necessary to reheat, use as low heat as possible, since sour cream and yogurt both tend to curdle when heated.

Serves four.

Pastel de Choclo (Chilean Sweet Corn Pie)

I cannot deny it—this recipe is work. Many of the recipes in this book are work. They call for chopping and dicing and grating and mincing. They call for two and three processes.

They call for an extended family. Maybe that's the way we'll live in the future. Maybe that's the way we should live now.

Pastel de Choclo brings warm memories from South America to me. There are many bad things going on in South America but the comfort and solace of extended families are two of the good things. You can chop and dice and grate and mince while talking—and laughing.

There are two distinct processes in making *Pastel de Choclo*. You have to make a sauteed hamburger and onion mixture; and you have to scrape fresh raw corn off the cob and cook it for a second mixture. The meat mixture goes on the bottom, the corn mixture on top, rather like a tamale pie, but very different. You'll see.

Meat Mixture

1 pound ground beef, lean

1 cup finely chopped onion

1 tablespoon oil

5 tablespoons hot water

1 teaspoon salt

½ teaspoon ground cumin

dash of black pepper

½ teaspoon paprika

pinch of ground cumin

dash of cayenne

pinch of ground oregano

In a skillet, brown the meat and onion in oil. Add hot water, salt, pepper, paprika, cumin, cayenne and oregano. Simmer, covered, for 30 minutes. Set aside, but keep warm.

Corn Topping

2 cups raw sweet corn, scraped off cob

2 tablespoons butter

1 cup milk

½ teaspoon salt

½ tablespoon fresh sweet basil, chopped (or ½ teaspoon dried)

1 teaspoon sugar

1 beaten egg

1½ teaspoons sugar, for sprinkling on top

1 hard boiled egg, sliced

¼ cup raisins

8 purple olives

4 pieces cooked chicken breast, deboned

To scrape corn from cob, cut with a sharp knife down each row of kernels. Then cut off tips of kernels. Finally, with the dull edge of the knife scrape the cob clean. When fresh corn is not in season you can use a can of cream style corn, then omitting the teaspoon of sugar in the cooked mixture.

Simmer corn with butter, milk, salt, basil and sugar until tender, about 3 minutes. Stir the beaten egg into hot corn mixture.

Place the hot meat mixture in a greased baking dish 3 inches deep. Distribute raisins, olives, slices of egg, and pieces of chicken across the dish. Spoon the corn mixture on top. Sprinkle with 1 ½ teaspoons sugar. Bake 30 minutes in preheated 350° oven. The top should be golden brown when it's done cooking. Serve immediately.

Serves four.

Caldillo de Pescado (South American Fish Soup)

This is a main dish. With salad and bread it is a complete meal. In Chile we used pieces of fish, generally the *congrio* (congor eel), bone and all, but fish fillets will serve quite well.

1 cup chopped onion

1 small clove garlic, minced

2 tablespoons oil

1½ cups water

2 tomatoes, sliced

4 potatoes, quartered

1 rib celery, sliced

pinch of oregano

⅓ teaspoon ground cumin

½ teaspoon salt

pinch of paprika

dash of pepper

¼ cup white wine

1 pound fish fillets

1 egg yolk, beaten

1 tablespoon chopped parsley

In a heavy pot, cook onion and garlic in oil until tender but not brown. Add all ingredients except fish, egg yolk and parsley. Simmer, covered, for 20 minutes. Add the fish and simmer 15 minutes more. Remove ½ cup of the broth and stir it into the egg yolk. Return this mixture to the pot. Heat gently. Add parsley and serve at once.

Serves four.

I stood still and listened to the world coming awake. A woodpecker was thumping on a tree. Small birds were calling and chirping, greeting the day. The lake was placid as a millpond. Here and there I could see a spreading circle that a fish made as it rose to the surface, maybe for a May fly even though this was June. A chipmunk scurried around, a pine squirrel scolded. I walked on. My feet didn't make a sound because I was walking on moss. So calm and peaceful. Like a corner of the world left out of all the hurley-burley. Is that why fishermen go fishing at five in the morning?

A Moment In Shangri-La

I never saw the mountain goats at all, but they were there. A photographer stood right beside me and said, "There are five mountain goats on that cliff." I looked but I couldn't see any. Even though mountain goats are not that hard to see. They're big and white and shaggy. I'm really quite near-sighted. But it was raining and the fog was thick. I was in Glacier Park on the high trail overlooking Hidden Lake.

I didn't mind at all not seeing the goats. In fact, I was very happy about it. They were part of an invisible mystery. I love invisible mysteries. In fact, that's why I was walking in the rain in Glacier Park. Actually I was looking for a plant called mountain sorrel. It's an edible wild plant used by the oldtime Indians and the early explorers. I wasn't going to pick it. I don't pick plants in national parks. I just wanted to look at it and think about it, about the good lemony taste the leaves have, and the high amount of vitamins A and C, and how this knowledge was used by the Indians long before the whites discovered a cure for scurvy. You know, we could have cured scurvy long before we did. The Indians knew all kinds of plants that were rich in vitamin C.

I found the mountain sorrel on the trail above Logan Pass and then I walked on toward Hidden Lake. Because of the fog and rain I had the trail practically to myself. It was like a small miracle. No noise, the huge cliffs towering above me, the green hanging valleys below, the white snowfields that hadn't melted from last year and probably wouldn't ever melt. New snow would fall on top of the old.

I stood on the cliff overlooking Hidden Lake and of course I thought of Shangri-La. The photographer was taking a picture of Shangri-La and the goats were living in it. Those goats had a valley all to themselves, a green valley with a blue lake and jagged mountain peaks to keep intruders out. And in winter, twenty, thirty, forty, or a hundred feet of snow! Wind and hail. Winter storms are so severe here that trees can't grow. The few that survive aren't trees at all. They are little patches of shrubbery all twisted and gaunt.

How do the goats survive? I don't want to know really. A Shangri-La should be a mystery. And once in a while we mere mortals should chance upon it. In the fog and mist, when people aren't there and it's quiet and you can't see very far.

So I had my moment in Shangri-La. My half a day. I came home and told everybody, "I didn't see the goats at all but I didn't mind."

"You nummy," they said, "why didn't you carry field glasses?"

I know, I should. But I smelled the goats. Right there on the cliff where I stood, looking down at Hidden Lake in that green valley. The goats must have stood on that same cliff. That's enough for me.

Whole Wheat Bread

I once weighed 160 pounds. I ate no bread, no potatoes. "Too fattening," I said. How could I have said a thing like that? I should have known better. I was a graduate of Cornell University's Home Economics College.

Bread and potatoes are not fattening. It's what you put on the bread and potatoes that is fattening. Everyone knows that, but we love to give up bread and potatoes when we're on a diet.

Good bread satisfies—its that easy. And a satisfied stomach doesn't have cravings. You can pass up the Danish, the chocolate chip cookies, the doughnuts.

½ cup warm water

2 tablespoons active dry yeast

¼ cup honey or molasses (or more to taste)

1 tablespoon salt

¼ cup oil

2¼ cups warm water

6 - 7 cups whole wheat flour

Measure warm water into a large bowl and sprinkle yeast over the water. Stir until yeast is dissolved. Stir in honey, salt, oil, 2¼ cups warm water and 3½ cups flour. Beat until smooth. Mix in enough of the remaining flour to make dough easy to handle.

Turn dough onto a lightly floured board. Knead until smooth and elastic (about 10 minutes). Place in a greased bowl, and turn greased side up. Cover with a clean cloth and let it rise in a warm place until doubled (about 1½ hours).

Punch down the dough and divide it in half. Roll each half into a rectangle 18 x 9. Roll up, beginning at short side. With side of hand, press each end to seal. Fold ends under loaf. Place seam side down in greased 9 x 5 x 3 loaf pans. Cover. Let rise until doubled (about 1 hour).

Preheat oven to 375°. Bake 40 - 45 minutes or until loaves sound hollow. Remove from pans. Brush loaves with butter if a soft crust is desired. Cool on wire racks.

Makes two loaves.

Thanks to Sheila Smith, Missoula, Montana

Mom Is Ninety-Two—What Is Her Secret?

I sent my mother an envelope of clippings about health. "Mom, eat whole wheat bread. Put bran in your hotcakes. Here are some exercises anyone can do."

My sister wrote back: "Mom is ninety-two years old. She must be doing something right."

I had to laugh. What was I doing? Giving advice to someone who is ninety-two years old and enjoying life. Mom eats three meals a day, walks to the store, writes letters to her seven children, whom she raised on a hard-rock farm in the middle of the Depression.

The purpose of Mom's walks to the store is to buy a fresh loaf of Vienna bread. You know what Vienna bread is— pure white. "Mom, eat whole wheat bread," I wrote. "It's much better for your digestion."

My church group hooted and hollered when I told them how I wrote to my mother. "At ninety-two you should ask her for advice!" they said. So I did. Mom wrote back: "I don't know." So I had to guess. I think it's because she has lived in an extended family all her life. First the children, then my sister came home with a grandchild. When my father died, Mom moved in with that same daughter, who is now remarried.

The husband had a widowed sister who also lived with them. "Four people in one house," you might say. "Impossible!" But it worked. My sister, when she wanted to be alone, retired to the attic. She has her typewriter up there. The husband has a little garden house hideaway in the yard. The widowed sister has the downstairs parlor. My mother has the upstairs veranda.

But they eat dinner together every night, leisurely. Everyone helps with the cooking and the dishes.

For Mother's Day, Mom will get a plant, two bouquets, a new bonnet and—how can I say this!—a box of chocolates. Maybe two boxes. Terrible! Well, she'll pass them around to anyone who comes to call. At ninety-two what can I say? That we should live so long!!

Huckleberry Coffeecake

Some years the huckleberry crop is sparse. Then one doesn't squander four cups on one baked item. I make pancakes, using only half a cup, or muffins, using one cup, or a coffeecake, using two cups.

2 cups all-purpose flour (sift before measuring)

2 teaspoons baking powder

¼ teaspoon salt

pinch of cinnamon

⅓ cup butter

¾ cup sugar

2 eggs, separated

⅔ cup milk

2 cups fresh huckleberries (blueberries)

Sift flour with baking powder, salt and spices. Set aside. Beat egg whites until stiff, and set aside.

In a large bowl, cream the butter, sugar and egg yolks. Add flour mixture to it alternately with milk, stirring until just blended. Stir in the huckleberries. Fold in the beaten egg whites. Pour into a greased 9-inch square cake pan. Bake in a preheated 350° oven about 35 - 45 minutes, or until done.

Sprinkle lightly with powdered sugar. Cut in squares. Serve warm.

Hungry Horse Huckleberries And The Aurora Borealis

That's the way I was one day this summer at Hungry Horse Reservoir. I was picking huckleberries. This year the crop was of such size and quantity all the bears in the world couldn't eat them up. My eyes bugged out at the size of the berries. Oldtimers have been telling me for years how big the Hungry Horse huckleberries get: as big as a cherry, as big as a grape. Now I believe! In fact, I'll probably add a few tales myself: so big it took two bites to eat one berry, so thick the mountainside was black. In truth, the berrying was so fantastic my friend Allison and I couldn't believe our good fortune.

Allison is the woman I talked about a few years ago, saying she lives in Montana because of the huckleberries. She is a *huckleberry hound!* She smells them before she gets to them. I'm getting that way too. I was hiking down the mountain the other day and suddenly I sniffed the air like a hound dog—no, like a bear—and I said I smelled huckleberries and sure enough, there off the trail down the cliff were fat ripe huckleberries. They'll be there until after Labor Day at that altitude.

When I stood in awe like an ancient it was at Hungry Horse the evening of the day I had picked these big as a house huckleberries. Allison and I were camped on top of a mountain overlooking the Hungry Horse Reservoir. It was just a day or two past full moon so we stayed up to watch the moon shining on the water. That was enough beauty. We didn't need any more. But on top of that, suddenly the sky was full of light. It was the aurora borealis, the Northern Lights. Neither Allison or I had ever seen a really full display. Well, how many people have? We live in cities. But here we were, by pure accident on top of a mountain without a manufactured light anywhere, and on comes the aurora borealis. Shooting streamers across the sky. Waves of light undulating like the ocean. Clouds of light playing back and forth. We just stood there. We had to back up against a tree to steady ourselves so we wouldn't fall over backwards.

"What did the ancient Indians think of this?" I said to Allison. "What did the Eskimos think?" Wouldn't they think the world was coming to an end?

They didn't have encyclopedias to look it up and know it was electricity or sun spots or something. Actually, I don't want to know what the aurora borealis is. I just want to remember that on top of a mountain overlooking Hungry Horse Reservoir in August, 1982, I was in the middle of something awesome and it was a privilege to be part of it and I say Amen.

I stood in awe. Sometimes you have to do that. When you're in the middle of something so big you have no way of understanding it. Like an ancient primitive you stand there, just stand there.

Montana Huckleberry Pie

Every 4th of July Mel bakes two huckleberry pies for the family reunion at Georgetown Lake. By now it's a ritual. The day wouldn't be complete without those two huckleberry pies filling the lake trailer with their aroma.

We get up early, bake the pies, put them in a cardboard box and off we go.

The huckleberries for the pies are not this year's crop. They have to be saved from last year because huckleberries in Montana aren't ripe until the middle of July. Mel and I think of it as our duty to save enough huckleberries to bake two pies for the 4th of July family reunion.

Of course it's also our duty to pick them. But that's no duty. That's a pleasure. Picking huckleberries in western Montana is like going to heaven.

It's hard to explain, really, what the magic is. I think perhaps it's the place where huckleberries grow. Picture a steep mountainside, with conifer woods above, and a green valley below. There's a river meandering through the valley. You are sitting in late afternoon sun on the edge of the deep green woods. Wind is soughing in the pine trees. Listen! It is the only sound you hear. Oh yes, there are some small birds calling and chirping, but they are musical notes that blend in with the soughing of the wind. The sun is hot but there's a breeze.

I could sit on that mountainside in the berry patch forever. This is as close to paradise as I can imagine.

Montana huckleberries are really blueberries. The scientific name of the genus is *Vaccinium* and that is the blueberry genus. But these wild berries are a world apart from the commercial blueberry so they deserve a distinct title. We Montanans will fight for the name "huckleberry".

4 cups fresh or frozen huckleberries (blueberries)

¾ cup sugar (more if berries are very tart)

3 tablespoons flour

pastry for double-crust 9-inch pie (do try whole wheat pastry flour)

Mix flour and sugar with berries. Set aside.

Roll out a little more than half the pastry dough to 1/8-inch thickness and fit into a 9-inch pie pan. Pour the berries into the pie shell. (If you use commercial blueberries sprinkle 1 tablespoon lemon juice on top.)

Roll remaining pastry a little thinner than for the bottom crust. Prick with your favorite design. Brush the edge of the bottom crust with cold water and place the upper crust on pie. Press crusts together at the rim and trim off the excess dough. Flute the edge.

Bake in a preheated 450° oven for 10 minutes. Reduce the heat to 350° and bake about 40 minutes.

Elderberry Muffins

I have to pick a quart of elderberries every year even though they're not one of my favorite wild fruits. It's a tradition from my childhood. Our farm had a spring and over the spring grew an elderberry bush (*Sambucus cerulea* or *Sambucus canadensis*). It shaded the spring, and the frog that lived in the spring. Imagine drinking water from a spring with a resident frog! We cleaned out the spring a million times but the frog was always there. It was more resident that we were because I'm sure it's still there.

The elderberries are in my memory so I make these muffins once a year. There's a pleasant crunch as you chew.

You may not have elderberries in your area. You can use blueberries, huckleberries or cranberries. If you use cranberries, chop them before adding.

1 cup whole wheat flour

1 cup white flour

1½ teaspoons baking powder

½ teaspoon baking soda

½ teaspoon salt

1 egg, beaten

1¼ cups plain yogurt

3 tablespoons melted butter

3 tablespoons honey

1 cup fresh elderberries

½ teaspoon grated orange rind

Combine the dry ingredients and set them aside. Then combine the wet ingredients and add them to the dry ones with a few quick strokes. The batter should be blended but lumpy. Overmixing makes tough muffins. Fold in the elderberries and grated orange rind last. Bake in preheated 375° oven for 25 - 30 minutes.

Makes about 24 muffins.

All backpack food has to be minus the water. That's what backpack food means — dried food. You add the water when you make camp.

Backpacking is so popular by now there are dozens of books on the subject of backpacking foods. I'll just give some favorite recipes of mine.

Trail Breakfast: Bulgur with Cheese

Both Mel and I like hot cereal for a camp breakfast. Some people carry dried eggs, some people eat granola with milk (made by mixing powdered dried milk with water, hot or cold.)

Mel mixes three or four kinds of grains for his breakfast, the base being oats and then adding a little wheat flakes, barley flakes, etc. I like bulgur wheat, which is cracked, partially-cooked, dried wheat. I buy the bulgur as finely ground as possible so it will cook to a cream-of-wheat consistency. If I can find whole wheat farina I buy that.

The law of backpacking is that each person carries her/his own food and her/his own pot, so Mel and I can vary our breakfast cereal to suit our individual tastes. Since our dried milk is non-fat I add richness to my cereal in the form of either cheese or peanut butter, both of which we carry as standard items. (See my recipe for Peanut-Buttery Cereal on page 162.)

½ cup bulgur wheat, finely ground

1 cup water

⅓ cup dried milk

2 tablespoons slivered cheddar cheese

Mix bulgur wheat, water and milk in cooking pan. Bring to boil. Remove from heat and let stand 10 or 15 minutes. This waiting time allows the wheat to soften on its own and you can use the camp stove for toasting bread or heating your partner's breakfast.

Return cereal to stove. Bring to boil, stirring constantly. Remove from stove, add slivers of cheese and stir until cheese is melted. Add salt if necessary for your taste.

One serving.

Trail Mix *(Gorp)*

Gorp is the "in" name for trail mix, and trail mix is the health food person's answer to the candy bar.

Trail mix has high energy value because it has dried fruits with all their natural sugars and it has nuts and seeds with their high oil content. But these are not empty calories. You have the vitamins, minerals and fiber of the whole, unprocessed foods.

Some gorp mixtures—in fact, many gorp mixtures—have small chocolate candies in them. I don't have candy in my recipe but you can add it if you must.

¾ cup roasted Spanish peanuts

1 cup lightly toasted sunflower seeds

¼ cup sliced almonds

½ cup raisins

¼ cup chopped dates

**¼ cup dried plums, apricots or
    cherries, cut up**

¼ cup dried banana slices

Mix together. Makes three and one half cups.

If you can remember to end your snack with peanuts, your teeth will be cleaned of the sticky fruit. You don't want to eat a healthful snack but cause yourself tooth decay.

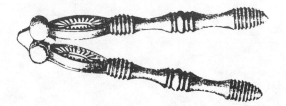

Roughing It Is Toughing It

I did it. I put my bed and my board on my back and hiked into the wilderness. At age 55. Oh, I've been in the wilderness before but only on day trips—five or six or eight miles in and five or six or eight miles out, taking along lunch and water canteen.

Putting your bed on your back is a whole different category. To sleep in the wilderness puts you in the packhorse category. Just the packframe is enough to scare you—all those clamps and straps and buckles.

You know how the knights in armor used to be hoisted on their horse? It's true—they were hoisted on their horse by a block and tackle. Well, a full backpack is like that. You need help to get it on your back.

I know—a person should go out with just a knife and blanket. That's what the survival courses teach. But what do you do if it rains? That's why backpackers have this tremendous pack. You can go out and suffer once or twice, but you don't want to be miserable all the time.

So you carry a tent, a fly—that's a waterproof covering over the tent, a stove to cook with since wilderness areas don't allow fires, pots and pans, eating utensils, a cold weather jacket, a wet weather jacket, sneakers or sandals so you can rest your feet out of your hiking boots, and food, of course—about two pounds per day.

You have to carry water, first aid equipment, a mosquito repellent. I don't use mosquito repellent—I'm trying herbs. None of the herbs are perfect but none of the mosquito repellents are perfect either. Some are so perfumed you have to walk one hundred yards ahead of or one hundred yards behind the people who use them. Others work in mild situations but not in a true bonafide mosquito attack.

It seems hard to believe that on my very first backpack, on my neophyte attempt, every adverse condition known to backpackers would come together on a weekend. The mosquitos were only one segment. I strained from morning to night. The trail was mud a foot thick. My feet weighed a ton. We had to cross eight creeks, hopping from stone to stone. A person loaded down like a muletrain is not balanced for hopping from stone to stone. I felt if I leaned just one inch sideways I'd go crashing.

We arrived at the lake and there were gnats in addition to the mosquitos. Some people retired to their tent, others built a fire—fires were allowed here—and sat in the smoke. We smelled like smoked salami from then on but the smoke did repel the bugs. Gnats get into your eyes behind your glasses and drive you crazy.

Will I ever go out again? With such an initiation? Loaded like a burro, rained on day and night—got up to look at the stars and sloshed around in the mud—ate dinner in a cloud of mosquitos, swallowed a gnat with the macaroni, had to put on wet boots in the morning—is there a worse feeling than soaking wet hiking boots at 6:00 a.m.?

Shouldn't I say never again? No, not at all.

I saw a lovely lake deep in the wilderness. It was emerald green and so quiet. Yes, I'll go again. It has to be better next time. I mean, it can't be worse.

Trail Dinner: Macaroni Plus

Lunch is no big deal on the trail. It's a quick meal because I am in a hurry to get my pack off and my boots off and be in a permanent camp for the night. Also the sun might be beating down on my head. Or the rain.

I eat bread and cheese, drink plain water, and for quick energy I chew on gorp. I chew slowly—it's better for my digestion. I don't want indigestion on the trail. I carry a thermos in my backpack and keep it full of hot water for herb tea, or instant coffee. Some people nibble on jerky, which is dried meat.

Dinner has to be substantial and good. Mel and I don't buy expensive freeze-dried meals. We like to think we can catch a fish for dinner. A fish fresh from the water, laid gently on red-hot coals, is the perfect camp dinner. I need nothing else. Well, maybe a piece of camp bread, heated over the coals. And some dried fruit, softened in warm water. We always carry dried plums and apricots.

Macaroni Plus is generally macaroni and cheese with dried vegetables and sometimes bits of edible wild plants gathered along the trail. We carry both whole wheat and white macaroni. "Why white macaroni?" you might ask. It's because there are times our

stomachs prefer white macaroni, especially when we have eaten a quart of huckleberries along the trail. We even carry—how can I admit it—instant mashed potatoes for just such a time. There are times you want nothing for dinner but soft, squashy instant mashed potatoes with milk and lots of margarine and cheese.

Don't let anyone tell you you have to throw away the water in which you cook macaroni. The first time I saved the water I held my breath to see if the sky was going to fall on my head—we are that accustomed to not questioning—but by now I not only use the macaroni or spaghetti water out camping, I use it at home too. What's the use of buying enriched macaroni or spaghetti and then throwing the vitamins and minerals down the drain? And out camping I'm certainly not going to lug calories up the mountain and then throw them away.

What Mel and I call camp bread is a standard whole wheat pita bread, but we make individual breads only four inches in diameter and we poke holes in them with a fork, so they are flat cakes instead of pitas with a pocket in them. They get hard in our backpacks but they toast up fresh as can be. We can cut them in half and make sandwiches or split them and toast them over a fire or the camp stove. We carry margarine in a small plastic—ahem—cold cream jar.

2 cups dried macaroni (mix whole wheat and white)

4 cups water

2 tablespoons mixed dried vegetables (buy them in a health food store or dry your own)

1 tablespoon dried chopped onion

1 tablespoon dried parsley

1 tablespoon dried textured protein made from soybeans (can be found at a health food store)

2 tablespoons margarine

salt and pepper to taste

¼ cup dried milk

⅓ cup diced cheddar cheese

Bring macaroni, water, dried vegetables, onion, parsley, textured protein and margarine to a boil in a large camp pot. Boil 5 minutes and remove from stove. Cover and let stand 5 minutes. This saves fuel. The macaroni keeps cooking just by sitting. You can shut off the stove or use it for other purposes.

Return pot of macaroni to stove. Cook a minute more if the macaroni isn't done. Add cheese. Mix powdered milk with a little water and add to pot. Stir until cheese is melted. Add salt and pepper to taste.

Serves two.

Fall is
Harvesting the Sun

Making Jam And Jelly

Making jam and jelly is saying thank you to nature. You go out and walk in the hills and mountains, you bring home part of those hills and mountains, and then you put your bounty in glass jars. With love.

And with sugar. But this is not the end of the world. You aren't supposed to eat jam and jelly like mashed potatoes, by stuffing it in. Jam and jelly is a concentration of the sweetness and goodness of the fruit. And fruit itself I consider the crowning glory of the plant. The plant has nurtured itself since early spring. It developed leaves, it developed flowers: all of this was a prelude to the fruit.

And we, you and I, have the honor of eating the fruit. Of course in botanical terms you and I, and animals and birds, are only agents in the dispersal of the seed. Dispersing the seed is what it's all about. The plant isn't interested at all in providing you and me with a sweet juicy tidbit.

So let's go ahead and make our jam and jelly as long as we know what we're doing. We are preserving, for winter, concentrated sweetness and flavor. Where did I hear that expression, "a dab'll do you"? Well, a dab of exquisite jam or jelly will do you.

I actually eat almost no jam or jelly. My husband likes one spoonful on his breakfast toast, which is dry toast without butter. My husband and I prefer fruit sauce. This is like applesauce but made of many different fruits—some domestic, some wild.

People are always surprised when they find my larder is ninety-five percent domestic fruit: applesauce, plum sauce, rhubarb sauce, canned pears, apricots, cherries. I follow my own advice: "Don't go through the outdoors like Attila the Hun." There's a lot more fruit to be found within the city limits than there is out in the hills. I'm a gleaner, a picker-upper, a let-me-help-you-harvest type. I have my pear lady, my plum gentleman, my apricot family. I ask politely, I help pick the fruit, I fill the boxes of the host, clean up the ground, then walk home with my portion on my back.

I also visit the Farmers' Market and buy overripe fruit. I love overripe fruit. I'm not canning fruit to win a prize at the county fair. I want the full flavor of fruit ripened in the sun. None of that plastic-covered half green fruit in the supermarket. My stomach isn't happy with that.

Blue Ribbon Trash

Can you imagine a time when you would be happy to find out that somebody had dumped a load of trash on your farm? I said that to my husband the other day. We were cleaning out the basement and I was counting my jelly jars. "If we need any more," I said, "we can visit the city dump."

"We will not," my husband said. "We'll buy them in a store."

"I couldn't possibly do that," I said, "but I might go so far as to buy them at a rummage sale."

Those people who grew up in the Depression will know right away why the thought popped into my head about getting jelly jars at a dump. I was thirteen when I won two first prizes on jelly at the county fair and the jars came from a load of garbage somebody dumped on our back woodlot.

I was walking home from school the back way. We had two entrances into our Rock Hill Farm. That's what our farm was — rocks and hills, but it had lots of wild berries. We could make all the jam and jelly we wanted, if we could afford the sugar and if we had the jars.

I was walking along thinking about the county fair, which would be the first week of September, and could I make some jelly to enter and maybe win a first prize of three dollars. A blue ribbon would come too but the money was more important because in those days we had to put a deposit on books in high school and I would be a freshman.

I couldn't possibly ask my mother to buy jelly jars. And our family didn't buy food in jars. We didn't buy peanut butter or relish or anything like that. All we bought was sugar and flour and salt and chicken feed.

So it was a miracle when I rounded a bend in our back road and there, just off the dirt road, was a load of garbage. Somebody overnight had dumped a load of garbage on our back woodlot.

Did I think it was a terrible thing? Certainly not. It was a Christmas present. I flew like a flash to that garbage pile and started poking around.

Jars all over the place. What a haul I made! Pickle jars, mayonnaise jars, peanut butter jars. I filled my lunchbox and loaded my arms and trudged home happy as a squirrel with a sack of nuts.

I made currant jelly, raspberry jelly and blackberry jelly. I packed the jars into a box and took the box to our neighbor, Mrs. Thomsen, who would drive her car to the fair and carry all the exhibits of our 4-H Club.

I said to Mrs. Thomsen, "Will the judges take off points because the jelly isn't in real jelly jars?" I knew what a real jelly jar was. There were pictures in our 4-H bulletin.

"I hope not," Mrs. Thomsen said.

They must not have. Otherwise I wouldn't have won a first prize on my jelly in the pickle relish jar.

And here I am, still thinking of dumps and rummage sales to get a supply of jars. It's ridiculous! But I don't know. I wouldn't have the same feeling if I bought the jars in a store. I'm right back to when I was thirteen. I smile just to think of it. I see that load of trash in my mind's eye, sitting in that back woodlot and it looks beautiful.

Blackcap Jam

Blackcap is black raspberry (*Rubus leucodermis*) and it actually tastes better as a jam than eaten out of hand. It might be one of the best wild berry jams there is.

Many people are making low-sugar jams. It is possible to have a thick jam with little sugar or honey. You can use a thickening agent such as agar-agar (a seaweed gelatin), or you can use a new type of pectin called low-methoxyl pectin. Ask for these products (with cooking directions) in health food stores.

To preserve the most vitamins I suggest uncooked jam. This type of jam can be thickened with unflavored gelatin and very little sugar and then you would call it diet jam.

Ordinary uncooked freezer jam does have a large amount of sugar. The recipe on the powdered pectin package calls for 4½ cups sugar to 3¼ cups crushed fruit.

Since I find only a quart or two of blackcaps per year I throw caution to the wind and make straight cooked old-fashioned high sugar and pectin jam. I put it in tiny, tiny jars and dole it out like gold.

Jam has the whole fruit in it. Jelly has only the fruit juice. When I pick wild fruit as hard to find as blackcaps, I don't want to throw any part of it away so I make jam.

6 cups blackcaps (black raspberries)

2 tablespoons lemon juice

4¼ cups sugar

½ package powdered pectin

Wash fruit, then grind or crush thoroughly. You should have a little less than 3 cups of crushed fruit. Add the lemon juice and if necessary, a little water, to make exactly 3 cups.

Put fruit and lemon juice in kettle. Stir in the powdered pectin. Bring to a boil, stirring constantly. Add sugar and stir well. Bring to a hard boil, stirring constantly. Boil exactly 4 minutes. Remove from heat.

Ladle into sterilized glass jars. Seal with wax, or use canning jars with two-piece metal lids.

Chokecherry Syrup

Fruit syrup is like maple syrup but the base is fruit juice instead of sap from the maple tree. It has a great deal of sugar. I regret to say chokecherry syrup has one and one fourth cups of sugar to each cup of prepared fruit juice. But you're not supposed to drink it like water. It's a delicacy.

Chokecherries have an exotic taste. Some people say the taste is just plain wild—rank. But the high sugar content smoothes the taste.

Chokecherry syrup is for pancakes or for ice cream. I put it away in the pantry and when a person has a cold I put a spoonful into a cup of hot water, add lemon juice and dose the patient. It's not as good at alleviating a cold as hot chicken soup with garlic and cayenne pepper but it's a change.

In South America fruit syrups were used to make punch at children's parties. That was before soda pop was made there.

Regardless of what recipe you use, your syrup will not turn out the same each time you make it. Fruit varies in acid content, in ripeness and in sugar content. I've made syrup, poured it into jars and the next day it was jelly. By accident I had the exact proportion of juice, sugar, acid and pectin. I've also made jelly—or what I thought was jelly—poured it into jars and the next day it was syrup. If this happens to you call it an adventure. Just change the labels on the jars and carry on.

1 gallon chokecherries

1 quart water

1 tablespoon lemon juice

2 tablespoons powdered pectin

**sugar to measure (1 ¼ cups per cup
of prepared juice)**

To prepare the juice wash the chokecherries, add the water and bring it to a boil. Then simmer about 25 minutes, or until the chokecherries are soft. Strain through a sieve, pressing gently so you have some pulp mixed with the juice. (The pulp gives body to the syrup.)

Measure the lemon juice into the kettle. Add pectin and stir well. Heat to a rolling boil. Boil for 1 minute. Add sugar, mix thoroughly, and bring back to a rolling boil for 1 minute.

Pour into hot canning jars, put on the lids, and process in a boiling water bath according to the instructions on the canner.

Rose Hip Preserves

"What happened to my rose hip jelly?" the letter said. "The spoon stuck straight up. I couldn't remove it."

It's not hard to have a fiasco with rose hip jelly. I've had several myself. The thing with rose hips, which are fruit of the rose bush, is this: you don't have all the ingredients for a proper jelly. You can add all the sugar in the world and cook until the cows come home but you won't have a jelly—you'll have a syrup, a thick honey. And finally, if you persist, as my friend Betty Raymond in Butte did, you'll get glue. Put a spoon in and you'll never get it out. I once boiled that stage over on an electric stove. The stove was never the same again.

Many people are happy with that honey-type rose hip jelly. When my husband and I were new in Chile and we were visiting the southern part of the country, where there are whole communities of German descent, we were invited to tea. Oh, what a lovely custom! Tea in the middle of the afternoon with hot bread and butter and jam or jelly.

In this German home the jelly came in a saucer and it was a bright orange, thick, honey-like preserve. "What's this?" I asked the lady of the house. She took me to the window and pointed to some wild rose bushes growing along the highway. "Oh" I said, "rose hips. Well, glory be." The preserve was delicious—a taste halfway between apricot nectar and clover honey.

It wasn't until Mel and I returned to the USA that I ever thought of making real jelly out of rose hips and then I had my second fiasco, even though I added pectin. I forgot to add something acid, like lemon juice or crabapple juice. A true jelly is a chemical compound with exact proportions of sugar, fruit juice, pectin and acid. Rose hips have no pectin and no acid. Betty cooked and cooked and still she got only a thick, sticky preserve.

I finally added the proper amount of lemon juice and the jelly jelled, but I wasn't too happy. When you use commercial pectin you have to add more sugar than you have fruit or fruit juice, so a jar of jelly or jam is sixty percent sugar.

I now freeze or can plain rose hip sauce (puree), unsweetened, and add it to soups, casseroles, and puddings. I even make rose hip tea out of it. Far more vitamin C is preserved this way than in dried rose hips.

But I do make two or three small jars of rose hip honey, just to bring back memories of southern Chile—miles and miles of wild rose bushes along the Pan American Highway, high tea in warm cozy cottages.

Rose Hip Puree

2 quarts rose hips, measured after the blossom and stem ends have been removed

5 cups water

Grind the rose hips. Place in a kettle with water (use glass, enameled or stainless steel kettle to lessen vitamin C loss) and boil 20 minutes.

Remove from heat. Let stand in a cool place for 24 hours. Rub through a sieve. The consistency should be that of applesauce.

This puree can be preserved for winter by putting it in canning jars and processing it in a pressure canner. It can also be frozen.

Rose Hip Honey

4 cups rose hip puree (see above recipe)

4 teaspoons lemon juice

3½ cups sugar

Boil until thick. It may take only 5 minutes, or it may take longer, depending on how thick the puree is.

Pour into hot, sterilized jars and seal airtight. Because of the high sugar content, rose hip honey does not need to be processed in a pressure canner.

October's Bright Blue Weather

I can't stay home a minute these days. It's October's bright blue weather and I have to be out from morning to night. Here in the Rockies we don't have the tremendous display of fall colors that New England has, but we're happy with what we have.

I'm combining the looking with my last fall gathering. I came home today with a small sack of Oregon grape berries. I picked them right outside the journalism building at the university. This is the tall Oregon grape *Berberis aquifolium*, which is the state flower of Oregon. People grow it in their garden as an ornamental shrub. That's what this plant is doing beside the journalism building.

I waited until now to pick the fruit because I thought—well, maybe somebody else wanted it. But I guess nobody did because here it is October and the berries are still there.

You'll notice I say berries instead of grapes. That's because Oregon grapes are not grapes. They are in the barberry family. But they look like tiny wild grapes and they taste like tiny wild grapes. Very sour. You wouldn't want to eat them just off the bush.

I'm going to make fruit juice and I'm going to donate the juice to the ninth grade class of Butte High School. They invited me along on an expedition to see the bald eagles gather in Glacier Park for their annual feeding on Kokanee salmon.

The class is going in a group and they've got permission to use a park service blind so we'll be very close to the eagles. It'll be a sight to see—hundreds of huge beautiful eagles swooping down to feed on the migrating fish.

It'll be in November and the weather may be rugged. But rain or shine or snow or hail, I'll be in that blind.

In between watching the eagles the class is going to look over the plants and trees and rocks of Glacier Park. My part is to point out edible wild plants. Maybe some mushrooms too.

The group is going to stay overnight in a school gym or church, and the teachers will do the cooking. I'm trying to think what else I can take along. Maybe some dried rose hips for tea. I'm picking and drying a supply right now. The biggest ones I have are from the Rugosa rose. Those are so big you can cut them in half and take out the seeds and hairs around the seeds.

There are still a few chokecherries along the river and some elderberries. Not many. Just enough to serve as an excuse to be outdoors.

I won't get any housework done this month. I want to visit every maple tree in town and see when its color is just perfect. And all the birches. I have to examine the sumac and the highbush cranberry and the red-osier dogwood.

The days aren't long enough. So I have to let the house go. Let the dust pile up and blame it on October's bright blue weather.

Plum Leather

Fruit leather is fruit puree or sauce dried into a flat sheet that feels like leather. It should be dry to the touch, but not brittle. It should be pliable. When it's done you roll it up like a jellyroll.

People who make fruit leather all the time find it so easy to make they sometimes forget that things can go wrong. Fruit leather can mold. It can be a sticky mess. It can burn fast to the cookie sheet. It can turn sour.

You can make fruit leather out of almost any fruit: apple, pear, peach, plum, apricot, banana, berries. You can use the fruit either raw or cooked, with or without sweetening. You have to mash the fruit into a puree. Soft fruits such as bananas can be mashed with a fork. Apples can be pureed in a blender or cooked in as little water as possible and then made into a sauce.

If the fruit is very juicy, strain off some of the juice and use it for a breakfast drink or fruit punch. Fruit leather is easier to make if the puree is not too runny. Berries are sometimes so juicy that you have to either strain off some of the juice or mix the crushed berries with mashed bananas to obtain more bulk.

You can dry fruit leather outdoors in the sun, in the oven, or in a food dryer. If you dry leather outdoors in the sun you have to bring it in every night. If you have flies in the vicinity you have to cover the fruit with cheesecloth. Some people have bees or ants. A friend of mine has magpies stealing his fruit.

The solution to all these pitfalls is to use a food dryer. You can buy a food dryer ready-made or you can build one yourself. Plans and directions are available in public libraries, county extension offices, energy conservation offices—almost anywhere you find community-minded people doing self-help projects. A solar food dryer might be your number one choice because it uses the sun for energy and the sun is free.

I'd like to see community organizations own dryers. Also grain mills so families could have freshly ground whole wheat flour. Also pressure canners, so you could take your garden and can it right there in a big kitchen, talking and laughing and having fun, instead of being up at midnight laboring by yourself.

But you might start with dryers. I'll never forget visiting a family in the country where they showed me a shelf of jars filled with, not canned, but dried vegetables. "There's our whole garden," the young man said. I saw peas, corn, tomatoes, zucchini, parsley, onions, carrots, cabbage—all dried and stored.

This family did it in the sun, but I've learned more vitamins are lost from drying in the sun than in the shade. Also, time is of the essence. You want to dry quickly. And of course, magpies won't steal your produce inside a box, so funneling the sun inside a ventilated box is a good idea—and that's what a solar dryer is.

Food dryers (you can call them dehydrators) can also run on electricity, gas or kerosene. A simple food dryer is your own oven. I use that. I set the temperature at 110° to 130°F. The maximum temperature you should use is 150°. Higher temperatures will cook or caramelize the fruit. A friend of mine tried to make banana leather in a hot oven and it baked fast to the cookie sheet. It was a mess. I prop my oven door open about an inch to allow the moisture to escape. This method takes about ten to twelve hours.

Plum leather needs no added sugar. By removing the moisture you concentrate

natural sweetness so the finished leather is like candy. (Like candy it can contribute to tooth decay. Eat peanuts after the fruit leather, and remember to floss your teeth.)

Apricot leather can also be made without added sugar, but you need ripe apricots, not those green ones often found in stores. Oh, the joy of sun-ripened fruit! Just thinking about it makes my fingers open and close, itching to reach and pluck.

Did you know that apricots actually grow in Montana? I couldn't believe it when I first arrived here. Of course it's an "iffy" proposition. Sometimes the trees don't give a single apricot for six or eight years in a row. But nobody promised us a rose garden. We don't expect it.

It's like our old farm when I was a child. We never sprayed anything yet we always had fruit. If the bugs got the peaches we ate pears. If the cherries were poor we ate plums or grapes. The apples always had worms but we always had enough. It may be that a day will come when we welcome a worm in an apple as a sign that the apple is safe to eat.

Plum Leather

4 pounds ripe plums

Wash and remove pits. If you want raw plum leather (which I prefer) put fruit through a blender. If you prefer cooked fruit, cook it first, and then mash it with a fork or put it through a blender.

Line a cookie sheet with plastic wrap. (Don't use waxed paper and don't use aluminum wrap. Waxed paper melts into the fruit and aluminum wrap welds itself to the fruit.) Spread fruit puree ¼-inch thick on the lined sheets. Set cookie sheets in a food dryer or in the oven at a temperature not lower than 110° and not higher than 150°. If the oven is used, prop the door open 1 inch.

Dry the fruit until it feels like leather. Another test is if you can peel it off the plastic. But don't bother to peel it off. Cool the leather, roll it up—plastic liner and all—and store it in an airtight jar. Some people store it in the freezer. If not stored in the freezer, check your fruit leather once a month to make sure it is keeping perfectly.

Hard To Part With Bounty

"What!" I said to my husband Mel. "Open that jar of apple butter? Now? Before there's even a blizzard? We just made that apple butter a week ago."

I said that, then we laughed. I wonder if all homecanner people and jellymakers are this way. Can you bear to open a jar after you close it? After you process it, seal it, label it?

I call this the "Midas in the Pantry" syndrome. It happens to me every year, starting in July and continuing right through Christmas.

And I don't even have a real pantry. All I have is shelves in the basement.

I'd like to hear from people who have a real pantry, a walk-in pantry. Tell me—do you allow anyone to touch your beautiful jars before a two-foot snowstorm maroons you?

Don't you have to sit and admire and exclaim? Look at those Flathead cherries! Look at those apricots from Oregon! Look at those pears that were so huge and juicy this year! Every jar in your pantry has a story connected to it. You can't just end that story.

My apple butter filled the whole house with the smell of cinnamon, cloves, apple cider. Mel and I took turns stirring the pot. "Plop, plop"—that's the sound of thick apple butter spattering the lid. Next year we'll try making apple butter in the oven. You can do it that way. You don't have so much "plop, plop" spattering.

After we filled and labeled the jars we had to find the proper spot for the apple butter on the shelves. Should apple butter be put with the huckleberry jam and crabapple jelly? Should it go with the canned pears, peaches, cherries?

We found a spot, then we had to admire everything all over again. All those colors, all that bounty, that harvest. It was prior to Thanksgiving, but we still had to give thanks.

How can I allow anyone to open a jar that means all that? It's my summer, my fall, in that pantry.

It's probably just as well I don't have a large beautiful walk-in pantry. Do you remember how King Midas sat at midnight sifting through his gold? I can see myself. It's midnight, snowing outside, and there's a light on in one room of the house—the pantry. I'm sitting on the floor admiring my glass jars: peaches, pears, cherries, plums—apple butter.

Would I ever open one? Would anyone ever get a taste? King Midas and Kim Williams sitting on their gold.

Red and Gold Split Pea Soup

It's lucky nasturtiums are in flower right into fall because no one wants to cook split pea soup in summer, and besides, the bright red and gold of the nasturtium blossoms fit so splendidly on a fall table. Nasturtium flowers contain vitamin C so you are feeding your health and your eyes at the same time.

Don't be surprised to find a pungent taste. Nasturtium is in the same general family as watercress. But the smooth richness of split pea soup asks for an exotic garnish.

If you are out of nasturtiums in your garden you can use marigold petals. Marigolds are also edible and the colors are the same—red-orange, yellow-gold. If you are out of flowers entirely a dash of paprika will do nicely.

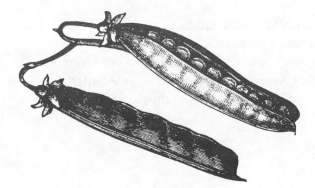

2 tablespoons oil

2 tablespoons chopped onion

1 clove garlic, minced

1 cup dried split peas

4 cups water

1 teaspoon salt

¼ cup chopped celery leaves

pinch of summer savory

1 potato, diced

½ cup grated carrot

1 rib celery, chopped

1 tablespoon chopped sweet red pepper

¼ cup chopped parsley

1 cup yogurt

¼ cup nasturtium flowers (petals only)

Saute the onion and garlic in oil in a large, heavy pot. Add washed split peas, water, salt, celery leaves and summer savory. Bring to a boil, cover, then simmer 45 minutes or until the peas are tender.

Add potato, carrot, celery, red pepper and parsley. Simmer 25 minutes. Serve hot with a dollop of yogurt and a sprinkling of nasturtium petals.

Serves four.

Carrot Peanut Loaf

Carrot Peanut Loaf is another good potluck dish. The peanuts enhance the carrot flavor. I use leftover rice for this dish because there is always leftover rice in my refrigerator. I always cook extra rice.

2 tablespoons butter

2 tablespoons minced onion

2 cups grated carrot

1 cup cooked brown rice

⅔ cup chopped raw or lightly roasted peanuts

¼ teaspoon salt

2 tablespoons chopped parsley

½ cup milk

2 eggs, beaten

Saute onion in butter. Add carrot and cook, covered, for 5 minutes. Remove from heat. Add other ingredients and mix. Place in oiled loaf pan. Bake in preheated 350° oven for 50 - 60 minutes.

Serves four.

Climbing Squaw Peak

It was raining and snowing and hailing. And there I was—a little green gnome toiling up the mountain. It was because of my New Year's resolution, which I made in September. Now that's not original with me. Lots of people do that. They say that fall is the best time to make resolutions. On New Year's Day it is enough to just survive. You're counting the days till the snow will go off the ground.

But in September and early October—oh, then you can make all kinds of resolutions. Your blood is surging in your veins. You look at a maple tree and it's bursting with glory, and you're bursting too—with something. A yearning maybe. Whatever it is, take advantage of it. That's what I said in September. I said I'm never going to be any younger—I'm 59 now. And there's my husband climbing all those mountains, standing on the peaks like—who was it standing on a peak in Darien and seeing the whole world spread out?

"Well," I said, "if I don't do it now I never will. I have to climb some of these peaks right now before I fall to pieces." I almost said, "before I'm stove up with arthritis," but I don't really know what "stove up" means.

Anyway, I said to my husband, "The Rocky Mountaineers are going to hike up Squaw Peak this Sunday but we can't go Sunday so why don't we go right now today."

"Are you capable?" he asked.

"Of course I am," I said, "but just in case, why don't you put a piece of nylon rope in your pocket so if I peter out I can sort of hang on to your belt and you'll help me up the mountain."

The day started out fine. It was so beautiful I could hardly stand it. We came to a clearing in the mountains and it must have been exactly the hour and the day and the minute. The whole clearing was full of red and orange and yellow. It was like a bowl in the mountains and it was filled with blazing red huckleberry and bronzey red fireweed. Two hundred acres of it surrounded by green pine trees. It was so beautiful we sat down and ate our lunch right then and there. While we were eating a white tail deer ran through the clearing. Through all that blazing color. A doe with her white tail high in the air.

It was pure magic. But then we went on. It started to rain. The rain turned to snow, the snow turned to hail. I had on the wrong kind of boots. They got soaked through. In fact, the water squished in and the water squished out. Luckily the rest of me stayed dry. My husband had an extra poncho. That's when I turned into a little green gnome. The poncho was so long it reached to my ankles and it had a hood that fell over my face. I had a staff to help me up the mountain and I put both hands on it and leaned into it. The mountain was that steep. Well, you can imagine the picture I made. I think that's what kept me going—my husband and I laughing at this little green gnome toiling up the mountain. Well, I made it up the mountain and I made it back down.

And I didn't catch pneumonia. Four hours with my feet soaked through. I guess it proves we're tougher than we think. It also proves anyone can do it. If a little old talker like me can climb a mountain in the rain and the snow at 59 years of age, anyone can do it. So go ahead. During this October go out and climb a mountain. And let me know how you make out.

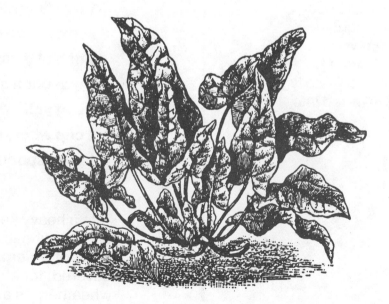

Lucy's Wheatberry Soup

The first time our Chilean housekeeper, Lucy, served this for Saturday lunch, my husband rose out of his seat in alarm. "My God!" he said. "She's feeding us CHICKEN FEED!"

She was. Lucy had cooked a potful of whole wheatberries, the whole kernels of wheat.

I thought the soup was delicious. It was rather like beef and barley soup except this was made out of wheat and it had a hambone instead of beef in it.

Mel ate a bowlful after he calmed down but he went around for weeks saying he'd been served chicken feed for Saturday lunch.

The marvel of wheatberries is that you preserve the most vitamin value. Vitamin E and some of the B vitamins are lost very easily after the grain is opened, when it is milled into flour or cracked for cereal.

½ cup diced onion

1 clove garlic, minced

2 tablespoons oil

1 cup wheatberries

7 cups hot water

1 hambone with about 1 cup meat attached

1 cup diced carrot

¼ cup diced sweet red pepper

1 rib celery, diced

1 cup finely shredded cabbage

½ teaspoon marjoram

pinch of thyme

1 teaspoon salt

1 egg yolk, well beaten

1 cup whole milk

1 tablespoon chopped parsley

In a heavy kettle, saute onion and garlic in oil. Add wheatberries and stir to coat with fat. Add hot water and the hambone. Simmer, covered, for about 2 hours, or until wheatberries are tender. Use of a pressure cooker will cut the time to 30 or 40 minutes. (I check after 30 minutes and then, if necessary, return to pressure for another 10 or 15 minutes.)

Add carrot, red pepper, celery, cabbage, marjoram, thyme and salt. Simmer 20 minutes.

Beat the egg yolk and stir 1 cup of hot soup into it. Return all to kettle, plus milk and parsley. Heat, but do not boil.

Serves four.

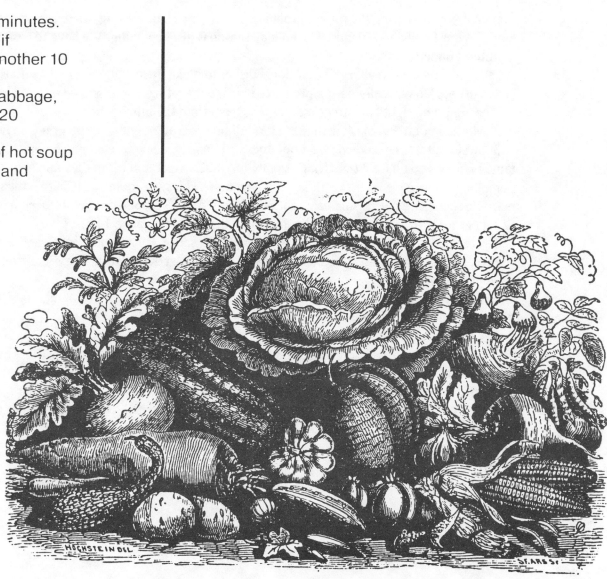

Towards A Healthier Thanksgiving

Even if you're serving the usual "groaning board" for Thanksgiving, there are ways to tone it down. I call it being kind to your family and friends. The holiday season is just beginning. We have to ease our digestive system into the marathon undertaking.

Let's see how we can alter the traditional dishes to make them a little more nutritious, a little easier to digest.

1. Turkey. Do we really need a pre-basted bird, one that has sugar and oil injected with a hypodermic needle? Many people are going right back to grandmother's fresh-from-the-butcher bird.

2. Mashed potatoes. Mash with just a taste of butter. You're going to use gravy anyway.

3. Sweet potatoes. Candied sweet potatoes with marshmallows are an abomination. If this dish is a tradition in your family I hope you phase it out. That's simply too much sugar and it's in the main course. How can you enjoy the pumpkin or mince pie if you've already eaten a dessert? If sweet potatoes baked in the skin aren't acceptable, try mashing them with a very small amount of butter and a tablespoon or two of frozen orange juice concentrate. Or try a sweet potato with apple casserole. I'm including that recipe on page 115.

4. Creamed onions. Instead of a thick heavy cream sauce, try a thinner sauce and sprinkle turmeric on top. Or omit the creamed onions and serve baked onions — baked in a covered dish. They retain all their flavor and need no seasoning at all.

5. Peas. I like frozen peas simply defrosted and warmed up, not cooked at all. They don't need to swim in butter either. Garnish with chopped chives.

6. Carrots. No sugar, please. Bake in a covered dish. Butter lightly.

7. Salad. Serve a tossed green salad or simply a relish plate. Please eliminate those colored gelatin salads that are all sugar and dye. People call them salads but they should be on the dessert counter. If you serve cole slaw try the old-fashioned vinegar and oil type instead of the pineapple-marshmallow-sweet-as-sugar type. Sauerkraut is a tradition with some families and that's fine because it aids the digestion. Dill pickles are another aid to digestion. Serve them instead of sweet pickles and sweet relishes.

8. Cranberry sauce has to be sweet because the berry is so acid naturally, but like pickles and sauerkraut, it is an aid to digestion. Actually the tart-yet-sweet taste of cranberry sauce is a welcome addition to the Thanksgiving feast — as long as the other dishes are not sugar-laden.

9. Stuffing. I know heavy stuffings are a tradition in many families. I prefer a lightly mixed bread, onion, herb stuffing, but you can't change too many things at one time.

10. Gravy. If you pour the fat off the roasting juices before making the gravy and make it quite thin you will do your guests a favor.

11. Pie. You have to have pie at Thanksgiving: mince and pumpkin (and huckleberry if you eat at the Williams' house). But you can lighten the mince pie by adding extra apple. Of course, there is the brandy sauce to consider. Well? If you must, you must. But allow people to say "No thanks," and serve them just a smidgin if they so desire.

Pumpkin pie, the traditional type, is a custard mix. You can easily cut down on the sugar and cream, and still have a firm, good-tasting pie. My family used milk to make the custard and put no whipped cream on top.

Everything about Thanksgiving is tradition. But don't forget, you are your children's tradition. You can ease away from some of your parents' and grandparents' customs, especially those pile-on-the-sugar-the-butter-the-cream customs.

I think some of the gilding of the lily came right after World War II. We homemakers were so tired of the wartime sugarless, eggless, butterless cakes that when the war ended we exploded into richness. The recipe books exploded the same way. I often think we could take most of our recipe books and cut the sugar and fat in half.

We have to learn to cook — and taste — without the hyped-up effect of over-sugaring, over-salting, over-creaming. It won't be easy. The children will surely say, "Ma, your chicken don't taste like the kuhnel's." But stand firm. Be kind to your fat-footed friends!

There's one other splendid idea that has taken hold — that of the potluck. Why should one person cook a whole Thanksgiving dinner? So OK, with potluck, the dinner might not be one hundred percent traditional. Oops! No candied sweet potatoes! Good!

I was talking to a student who said he'd moved to town only five days before Thanksgiving. All he had was a bare floor. But on Thanksgiving day he had five people sitting on that floor. Everyone brought something. Not a turkey. It was a very unorthodox Thanksgiving dinner. Pizza, I believe. But everyone ate. And they sang. The student had a guitar.

One of the best things about a potluck — aside from the fact that the hosts don't have to kill themselves — is the interesting conversation that comes along with the food. Why did we choose to bring this certain dish? Has it a meaning in our family? Did it come from a sojourn abroad? A potluck in a diverse group brings offerings not only with love but with landscape.

Thanksgiving Menu

When Mel and I have venison for Thanksgiving we're celebrating not only the Montana hunting and fishing tradition, but also the original Pilgrim Thanksgiving. I bet almost everyone thinks the first Thanksgiving was turkey, cranberry sauce and pumpkin pie. It wasn't. According to a letter written by a Mr. Edward Winslow on December 11, 1621, the three-day feast shared by Indians and colonists contained not one of those three ''traditional'' foods.

These were the foods: venison, goose, duck, shellfish, eels, white bread, cornbread, watercress, leeks, other sallet (salad) herbs, wild plums, dried berries, wine. Wild turkey was available, as were cranberries and pumpkins, but they didn't happen to be part of the feast.

So I'm very happy serving venison. The idea of cooking in beer came from a hunting friend of Mel's. I was a little taken back at first but the beer seems to tenderize the meat and it does no harm to the flavor.

We serve the venison with potatoes, carrots and onions, cooked in the same pot. Cornbread comes hot from the oven. A relish plate of green onions, celery and radishes is on the table, also a dish of cranberry sauce.

I cut the sugar in the cranberry sauce to one cup per two cups of fruit rather than what the recipe on the cranberry package calls for, which is equal amounts of sugar and fruit.

Dessert is a choice of huckleberry pie (which Mel makes), and either a mince or pumpkin pie which is generally brought by a guest.

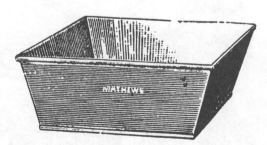

Venison Pot Roast

3-pound venison roast

4 cloves garlic

sprinkling of black pepper

2 tablespoons oil

1 bay leaf

1 rib celery, diced

¼ teaspoon sage

¼ teaspoon thyme

1 can beer (imported, chemical-free,
    if possible)

4 potatoes

4 carrots

4 onions

1 tablespoon chopped parsley

Insert garlic cloves into meat by poking tiny holes in meat with point of knife. Sprinkle meat with pepper. In a Dutch oven, heat oil and brown meat on all sides.

Let the pot cool. Add bay leaf, celery, sage, thyme and beer. Cover. Cook in 275° oven for 3 hours.

Add potatoes, carrots and onions. Cook about 1 hour longer, or until vegetables are tender.

Thicken liquid with flour if desired. I like this pot roast without thickening. Sprinkle chopped parsley on vegetables just before serving.

Serves four (with plenty of leftover meat).

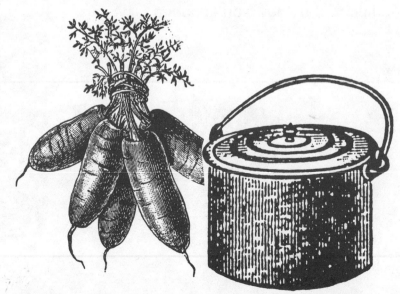

Sweet Potatoes with Apples

This is a good holiday potluck dish for people who like a dish with a sweet taste but prefer the sweetness to be as natural as possible.

You can use either yams (which are usually sweet potatoes botanically speaking) or true sweet potatoes in this recipe. What we call yams are generally a softer, sweeter, darker orange sweet potato. But whatever they are called, they are nutritious food. They are high in calories but the calories are not empty. The amount of vitamin A is like that of carrots, spinach and winter squash: an ordinary serving will give you your day's requirement. And since I consider vitamin A just as important as vitamin C in preventing colds and keeping generally healthy, I put green and yellow foods high on my list.

Mel and I bake ten pounds of sweet potatoes in one oven load. (We do the same with winter squash.) Then we let them cool and store them in the refrigerator or freezer. We keep an on-going supply of these vitamin-rich, naturally sweet foods.

Sweet Potatoes with Apples is practically a dessert in my estimation.

4 medium-sized sweet potatoes, baked

3 tart apples

2 tablespoons butter

½ cup orange juice

Slice into a buttered casserole dish alternate layers of sweet potatoes and apples 1 inch in thickness. (To peel or not to peel is up to the cook.) Dot the top with butter and pour orange juice over all. Bake, uncovered, in preheated 350° oven for 30 minutes.
Serves four.

Yogurt Cornbread

1 cup flour

½ teaspoon baking soda

1½ teaspoons baking powder

1 tablespoon sugar

½ teaspoon salt

1 cup cornmeal

1¼ cups yogurt

1 egg

3 tablespoons oil

Sift flour with baking soda, baking powder, sugar and salt. Add cornmeal.

In a separate bowl beat the egg with yogurt and oil.

Make a well in the dry ingredients. Add liquid mixture all at once and stir lightly but quickly. Don't overmix. Pour into greased 9-inch square pan. Bake in preheated 425° oven for about 30 minutes.

Sopapillas (South American Pumpkin Fry Bread)

You can use a little of your Halloween pumpkin to make this South American Pumpkin Fry Bread. It is not a health food recipe. How can fried bread be a health food recipe? It's a celebration recipe, like Indian Fry Bread served with Venison Stew at a powwow (see page 166).

South American Pumpkin Fry Bread celebrates the first rain of fall. In Chile we celebrated the first rain of fall because the summer was a long, hot, dry season. So this gentle rain would come and we would say ''Hallelujah!'' and we would gather together to make fry bread and have tea on a rainy afternoon.

We served sandwiches first: avocado, egg salad, tuna, hot melted cheese. The sopapillas were the dessert, served with a very special syrup, *miel de palma*, the syrup of the honey palm tree. Unfortunately, the demand for the syrup exceeded the supply and the tree became scarce. By now I imagine sopapillas are served with USA-style pancake syrup.

The original recipe calls for lard and no baking powder, but not even my Chilean friends make it that way any longer. You'd need years of practice and, as the saying goes, ''a hand with dough.''

1 cup flour

2 teaspoons baking powder

3 tablespoons butter

1 cup hot mashed pumpkin (or winter squash)

¼ cup milk (depends on how watery the pumpkin or squash is)

Sift flour and baking powder and set aside. In a separate bowl mix the butter into the pumpkin. Add milk and stir.

Add flour to pumpkin mixture. Mix lightly and then turn dough out on a floured board. Knead lightly for 30 seconds. Add more flour if necessary. You want a dough that you can roll out without sticking.

Roll the dough 1/8-inch thick. Cut into rounds with a 1-inch cookie cutter. Poke 3 holes in each round with a fork. Deep fry at 375°. (If you don't have a frying thermometer, the test is to fry a 1-inch cube of bread. When the cube fries in exactly 1 minute, the fat is the proper temperature.)

Serve with hot syrup.

Makes ten 2-inch sopapillas. Serves four or five people.

Pumpkin Bread

Pumpkin time means you need recipes to use up what's left of the Halloween jack-o'-lantern or the ten-pound bargain you bought at the Farmers' Market. Pumpkin time is also PTA meeting time and political campaign time. Crackers and cheese will fill the bill for some of the meetings but at other times there is no solution but a sweet treat.

I've been experimenting with cutting down on sugar in baked goods and it can be done. You might have to work up to it gradually so your family doesn't get a shock. You can certainly cut out the frosting. That's one of the virtues of pumpkin bread (also banana or date nut bread). No one expects frosting and you can cut down on the sugar, or honey, and the oil. There can be considerable nutritional value in these breads. Actually, they are not breads in the true sense. They are a cake, but we won't argue over that. The point is to add nutritive value and cut down on empty calories. Pumpkin (or squash) adds nutritive value.

Some people argue that you will not have perfect texture in cakes, cookies and so-called breads if you cut down on the sugar and fat. It may be so, but do we need perfect texture? It's like having a perfectly shined floor. Do you really want to use your life making a perfectly shined floor?

What we need is baked goods that have the most nutritive value possible and taste good, but that are low in fat and sugar. Now that's what I want to see earn first prizes at county fairs.

1¾ cups flour

2 teaspoons baking powder

½ teaspoon cinnamon

½ teaspoon nutmeg

½ teaspoon ginger

pinch of ground cloves

⅓ cup butter or margarine

¾ cup sugar

2 eggs, well beaten

1 cup cooked, mashed pumpkin

¼ cup milk

½ cup chopped walnuts or pecans

¼ cup lightly toasted sunflower seeds

Sift flour with baking powder, baking soda, cinnamon, nutmeg, ginger and cloves. Set aside.

In a large bowl, cream butter with sugar. Mix in eggs and pumpkin. Add milk. Stir in dry ingredients in 3 portions, blending until smooth after each addition. Add nuts and sunflower seeds. Pour into a greased bread pan (8½ x 4½) and bake in a preheated 350° oven for 1 hour, or until done.

Cowpie Cookies

Back to school and time for cookies. You might think that those of us who are using whole wheat flour and cutting down on white sugar would have a hard time making a tasty cookie. Not at all. Whole wheat flour takes naturally to many flavor combinations.

One combination—I found it in an old issue of *Organic Gardening* magazine (October, 1980)—is orange peel, honey and cinnamon. Another combination is date, nut and raisin. You can omit white sugar entirely and use honey. Brown sugar has no great virtue because generally it's only white sugar sprayed with a small quantity of molasses.

The recipe I'm including uses whole wheat flour and molasses. It's high in calories but nutritious. This is not a tea party cookie. The recipe came from a graduate student at the University of Montana, John Pierce. He goes hiking in the mountains pursuing his botany studies. He needs sustenance. As did his great-great-grandmother who made these cookies while going across Kansas in a covered wagon. "Somewhere it's written down how many buffalo chips it took to bake a batch of these cookies," John told me.

The reason John's cookies are called Cowpie is quite obvious when you see them. They are the right size, shape and color. And what's more, John piles one on top of another so they sort of stick together. Do you get the picture?

You'll find the list of ingredients quite different from your usual molasses cookie. These are the ingredients you would have in a covered wagon going across the prairie.

1 tablespoon baking soda

1 cup warm water

1 heaping tablespoon ginger

pinch of salt

2 cups molasses (use 1½ cups unsulfured and ½ cup blackstrap)

1 cup oil

4 cups whole wheat flour

In a mixing bowl dissolve baking soda in warm water. Add ginger and salt. Add molasses and oil. Mix. Add flour and mix thoroughly.

On a greased cookie sheet place large globs of dough, then flatten to ½-inch thickness by patting with a spoon dipped in water. Bake in a preheated 350° oven for 12 minutes.

Makes 30 cookies six inches in diameter.

How To Live On A Limited Income

I'm answering a letter I received from a woman in Kalamazoo. She wanted ideas on how to live on a limited income. Here are my ideas:

1. Don't let fashion dictate to you. I buy all my clothes at church sales. Sometimes people give them to me. I don't mind at all.

2. My husband and I, and my group of friends and I, enjoy little things in life. We keep watch on nature—birds building nests, clouds, earthworms, leaves on trees. Nature is free. We walk instead of riding so we can feel the earth.

3. Food. We don't buy steak and lobster. We take classes in how to cook with beans and peas and lentils so they taste good. We use lots of vegetables—baked squash, carrots. We thank people who have extra produce in their gardens and pass it on to us. We do favors for them in return. We use dandelion greens and other wild greens. My husband is a hunter and fisher so we have fish and meat, but I can cook and eat without any meat at all. We bake all our own cookies, desserts, most of our bread. We buy no prepared food.

4. Entertainment. We play cards with neighbors, go for walks, put together potluck dinners. One group has vegetarian potlucks; another has salad potlucks. Every community has free lectures, art receptions, sometimes movies. The public library is there for everyone. Leave your home and go to the public library and read there. Bring home books and magazines.

5. We do volunteer work in the community. This gets us out of the house. We meet people, we talk and laugh and have get-togethers with the other volunteers. Nobody should stay home alone too much.

6. Gift giving. I don't get involved in gift exchanging. I send little notes at all times of the year. I dry herbs and pass them around. In the fall when fruit is falling off the trees I make fruit leather out of plums, apricots, apples and pears and pass that along. I offer to make jam or jelly for people who have the fruit and sugar but are too busy to make the preserves.

7. In our group we go to school. We take classes. Some classes are free. It's fun. You meet new people, you are involved, you are learning. Learning keeps you young.

8. We exercise. People who live long healthy lives exercise. Get your heart beating faster for fifteen minutes every day. You feel good after you exercise—peppy, enthusiastic.

9. Don't sleep too much. It can get you down. Walk. Talk. Play cards. Teach something to somebody. Write your memoirs.

10. Don't burn up your money by keeping your house too warm. Wear long underwear. They have nice flowered ones nowadays. Exercise. Drink lots of hot herb tea. Wear pants. And a scarf on the head.

11. Share your house. On a limited income one person cannot keep a house. Two people can. And it's friendly.

Well, those are my ideas. I sent them to the woman in Kalamazoo. Maybe they'll help.

Granola Grabbies

"I enjoy Halloween just as much as the kids do," Nancy says. "I dress up like the Wicked Witch of the West, scare everybody to death, then I put the candied apples on the other end of a black thread maze like a spider's web and the kids have to go through the spider's web to get the apples."

That's the secret of a good Halloween—have the adults right in the middle of it enjoying it along with the children. Nancy can give candied apples because she knows the children who come to the door and they know her.

In fact, the parents come along with the children. It's a neighborhood Halloween. With that kind of trick-or-treating, you can make homemade goodies. You can make the kind of treat called "good goodies"—raisin oatmeal cookies, date nut bars, or popcorn balls.

I got the idea of Granola Grabbies from some school children who dropped in one day when I was making granola. They watched with interest and of course sampled the finished product. "Yum, good," one boy said. "I wish I could take it to school."

"Why can't you?" I asked.

"Aw," he said. "It's like eating chicken feed out of a sack."

I got the point. I had to stick the granola together. I did—with peanut butter.

2 cups granola*

½ cup raisins

½ cup chopped pecans

½ cup chopped dried apricots

1 cup dried skim milk

⅓ cup honey

1 cup (or more) non-hydrogenated, creamy peanut butter

½ cup roasted Spanish peanuts, ground or crushed into meal

Mix granola, raisins, pecans, apricots, dried milk and honey. Add peanut butter, a half cup at a time, until you can form small balls of the mixture with your hands. Add more than 1 cup of peanut butter if necessary.

Roll the balls in the peanut meal and then wrap them individually in squares of waxed paper. Serve at room temperature.

Makes about 36 small balls.

*See recipe page 126

Breakfast Granola

I wish to state right here that I do not deserve the name "Granola Grinder." This name was given to me by a group of high school students when I rode with them one November to Glacier Park to view the bald eagles feeding on the Kokanee salmon. The kids called the name a CB monicker.

Well, I might be a granola, as the jargon goes, but I really don't eat much granola. I don't even like it. I like my peanuts plain and simple, my sunflower seeds plain and simple, and I eat my oatmeal cooked—well cooked, so well cooked it's creamy.

But granola does have its place. It's high energy, concentrated food. Out backpacking you need quick energy to get yourself up the mountain with your thirty or forty pounds on your back. If you have to be on the trail at 6:00 a.m. and it's raining, you can manage to swallow a handful of granola and be on your way.

But I still cut down on the amount of honey and oil in my granola, compared to most recipes. I'm simply not happy with a candy-like granola.

I call my mixture Breakfast Granola. If you want a candy-like granola, just double the amount of honey and oil and add one cup of chopped dates.

2 tablespoons water

3 tablespoons oil

⅓ cup honey

1 teaspoon vanilla

1 teaspoon cinnamon

4 cups rolled oats

1 cup raw wheat germ

½ cup chopped raw almonds

¼ cup chopped raw cashews

⅔ cup roasted soybeans, chopped

1 cup lightly toasted sunflower seeds

⅔ cup roasted Spanish peanuts, chopped

⅔ cup raisins

Place in a large saucepan and heat (but do not boil) water, oil, honey, vanilla and cinnamon. Mix well.

Add oats, wheat germ, almonds and cashews. Mix thoroughly. Spread mixture in a roasting pan and bake in preheated 300° oven for about 40 minutes, stirring thoroughly every 10 minutes, and watching carefully so mixture does not burn.

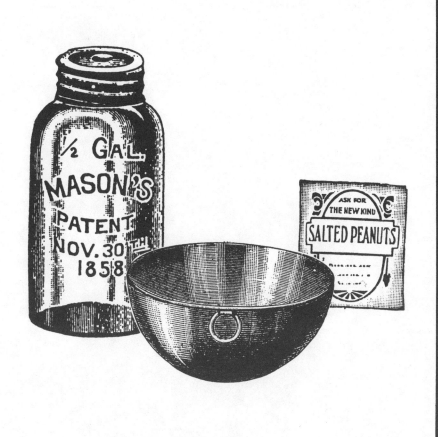

Remove from oven. Add soybeans, sunflower seeds, peanuts and raisins. Mix. Cool, then store in airtight jar in cool place. Use within a month or store in the refrigerator. Wheat germ can get rancid.
Makes nine cups.

Winter is
an International Kitchen

Cazuela de Ave (South American Chicken Soup)

I first tasted this chicken soup thickened with egg yolk and ground walnuts at an *hacienda* in the foothills of the Andes Mountains. The broth was so delicious I had to ask the host what the secret was.

My Hungarian mother made chicken soup practically daily, starting with the same kind of whole chicken, with the same rather—ahem—tough quality, but it was not in my mother's tradition to use any thickening agent.

The typical chicken in Chile is not padded with fat so the Chilean soup is lean (which of course is much better for our health) and the flavor, enhanced by good barnyard scratching, is excellent.

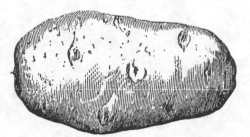

a 3-pound stewing hen

2 tablespoons oil

1 medium onion, quartered

½ cup chopped celery leaves

1 teaspoon oregano

1 teaspoon salt

10 cups water

1 carrot cut in four chunks

4 small potatoes

3 tablespoons rice

1 cup sliced fresh or frozen green beans

1 egg yolk

2 tablespoons ground walnuts

1 tablespoon chopped parsley

Cut up the chicken and brown pieces in oil in a large pot. Add onion, celery leaves, oregano, salt and 10 cups of water. Bring to a boil, cover and simmer until chicken is tender, about 20 - 30 minutes.

Add carrot, potatoes, rice and green beans. Simmer until vegetables are done. Beat egg yolk and put it in a soup tureen. Pour hot soup over the egg and stir. Add ground walnuts and chopped parsley. Serve at once.

Serves four.

Cazuela de Vaca *(South American Beef Soup)*

Cazuela de Vaca could be called either soup or stew. It's a hearty meal, as filling as New England boiled dinner. The usual version in South America is made with beef short ribs, bones and all. Each plate receives a big chunk of this bony, fatty meat, plus one potato, a chunk of pumpkin or squash, a piece of carrot, a piece of onion, and a few julienne-cut green beans. The broth is not thickened with flour. A few grains of rice are cooked along with the other ingredients. Sometimes a beaten egg yolk is added just before serving.

When we lived in Chile this dish was a staple of the working class. Today I can't say for sure, because the price of meat, even bony, fatty meat, might be prohibitive for the working class.

The ingredients you'll find different in this beef soup are chunks of winter squash and chunks of corncob. This corn on the cob in pieces is so important to the soup that a young Chilean, coming to visit us in winter, brought a can of the corn with him all the way from Santiago, Chile.

I'll admit it's very strange to find corncob pieces in your soup. ''How am I going to eat it?'' you'll ask. It isn't easy. You can use your knife and fork or, *en familia,* you can pick up the chunk and chomp on it.

1 pound stew meat

1 tablespoon oil

4 cups water

1 teaspoon salt

1 large carrot, cut in four pieces

4 medium-sized potatoes

4 chunks winter squash

1 ear fresh or frozen sweet corn, cut in four pieces, cob and all

½ sweet red pepper, cut in four slices

¼ cup chopped celery leaves

1 rib diced celery

½ teaspoon oregano

3 tablespoons uncooked rice

3 tablespoons chopped parsley

½ cup sliced green beans (fresh or frozen)

In a large, heavy pot, saute the meat in oil. Add water and salt. Bring to a boil, cover, and simmer until meat is tender.

Add all other ingredients except green beans and parsley. Simmer until potatoes are almost done. Add green beans and simmer until they are done. Add parsley and serve at once.

Serves four.

What To Do For A Cold

I felt like a Jewish grandmother but I did it anyway. My neighbor had a bad cold and I trotted over with a bowl of garlic soup.

"Glory be," she said. "It will smell up the house."

"That doesn't matter," I said. "Drink it boiling hot, then pull the blankets up to your nose, and sweat the cold right out."

"I'm taking these pills," she said.

"Well, take them if you like, but drink this soup first."

The soup wasn't just garlic. It was a chicken soup with garlic in it. The soup was made from a real chicken, simmered for hours with celery stalks, parsley, onion and sage. I removed the stock, added chopped garlic to it, and simmered it five minutes to slightly cook the garlic.

Hot chicken soup does help a cold. If you want to be technical you can say the soup "alleviates the symptoms." If you want to be non-technical—well, it just makes you feel better.

I like my chicken soup hot in two ways: hot from the stove and hot from chili peppers or cayenne. There seems to be scientific evidence that hot pepper helps clear the bronchial tubes. Again, you can omit scientific language and go with the idea that the hot soup-hot pepper mixture simply makes you warm all over and that works toward clearing a stuffy nose.

I'm a firm believer in the sweat-it-out theory. I mean, stop the cold before it has settled deep into your system. There's usually a point where you feel worn out, done in, achey; but you're not yet sneezing and coughing. That's the time to nip the cold.

That's when you start the hot soup regime. I use the hot soup in addition to a good meal, not in place of. I know some people starve a cold. I don't believe you can fight a cold on an empty stomach. I say eat a normal meal with fresh fruit and vegetables, yogurt, whole grains, good protein. Then drink your hot soup with hot pepper and garlic, and go to bed.

When I went over to my neighbor's this morning, I also took along a stocking cap and a pair of white cotton socks. I believe in keeping your head and feet warm. What's the use of drinking boiling hot soup which will make you sweat and will make your nose run if you don't hold in the heat?

My neighbor laughed but she put the cap on her head and the white cotton socks on her feet. I wrapped a scarf around her neck and piled on an extra blanket. Luckily she had on a cotton flannel nightgown or I would have had to go home and get one of those too. Synthetic fiber is not what you want when you need a comforting touch. Synthetic fibers are nervous. Cotton is a tranquilizer.

You don't have to believe all this. What works for one person doesn't work for everyone. I believe in garlic, chili pepper, hats and white cotton socks.

Garlic Soup

The difference between an ordinary chicken soup and garlic soup is a large quantity of garlic. Ordinary chicken soup has one or two discreet cloves of garlic. Garlic soup, the kind that you are going to take to your neighbor who has a bad cold, is loaded with garlic. It reeks of garlic. That doesn't matter. Good chicken soup with lots of garlic, onion and cayenne pepper will help relieve the symptoms of a cold.

The Basic Stock

1 stewing hen

3 quarts cold water

2 cups celery trimmings (leaves and tough ends)

½ cup chopped onion

1 clove garlic

1 bay leaf

½ teaspoon fresh sage, chopped (or ¼ teaspoon dried)

1 carrot, chopped

¼ cup chopped parsley

Place all ingredients in a heavy pot and heat to simmering. Skim off the foam that forms on top of the water. Simmer, partially covered, for 2 hours.

Allow stock to cool, then remove layer of grease which will have hardened on top.

Some people use only the stock, but I use everything in the pot.

Garlic Soup

2 cups strained chicken stock

5 cloves garlic, peeled and chopped

pinch of cayenne pepper

Place all ingredients in pot and simmer for 5 minutes. Serve steaming hot.
Serves one.

Saturday Soup

For my Hungarian parents a meal without soup was like a train without an engine. It couldn't go anywhere. Of course you have to remember, in the days when that custom started, people weren't drinking coffee with the meal. Nor milk, tea, orange pop, root beer, lemonade. And the houses weren't really heated. Hot soup warmed your stomach—it warmed your whole self. You could go on to enjoy your meal with zest and enthusiasm.

On days that my mother served meat and potatoes, the soup was chicken or beef bouillon, ladled out of the perennial soup pot. On other days the soup was the whole meal.

This Saturday Soup, made with all the week's leftovers, is a complete meal.

2 quarts vegetable stock

1 cup leftover beans

1 cup leftover spaghetti

1 cup shredded cabbage

1 cup diced carrot

½ cup corn, fresh or frozen

1 medium onion, diced

1 rib celery, chopped

2 fresh tomatoes, chopped (or 1 cup canned tomatoes)

1 tablespoon fresh basil leaves, chopped (or ½ teaspoon dried)

½ teaspoon thyme

Vegetable stock is all the juices you have saved from cooking vegetables all week: from carrots, peas, potatoes, corn, zucchini, etc. You can save these in empty milk cartons, stored in the refrigerator or freezer.

Put all ingredients in a large pot, bring to boil, cover and simmer 40 minutes.

Serve with large slices of freshly baked whole wheat bread and chunks of good cheese.

Serves six.

Paraguayan Dry Soup

This dish is not a soup at all. It's a corn, potato and cheese souffle—more or less. I don't know why it's called a soup. Our host in Paraguay called it that.

We were invited to an *estancia* where we admired the greenhouse filled with orchids, walked under mango and guava trees, drank a terrible cocktail made out of sugarcane brandy, and studiously avoided any talk of politics. I wrote in my notebook, "Land of red dirt and slow time."

2 tablespoons chopped onion

4 tablespoons butter

1 cup fresh or frozen sweet corn grated right off the cob

¾ cup milk

3 cups hot mashed potatoes, unseasoned

1 teaspoon salt

dash of pepper

2 tablespoons flour

1 tablespoon finely chopped parsley

4 ounces grated cheese

2 eggs, separated

Cook onion in butter for 3 minutes, until it is tender but not browned. Add corn and milk and cook 5 minutes. Remove the skillet from the stove.

Add the potatoes, salt, pepper, beaten egg yolks, flour, parsley, and grated cheese. Mix.

Beat egg whites until stiff and fold into the hot mixture. Pour into a greased baking dish and bake 30 minutes in a preheated 350° oven.

Serves four.

Pure Mountain Air

Fishing through the ice at Georgetown Lake may be a cold proposition but wait until you taste a fried Kokanee salmon. The lake is full of these fine fish and they taste just like the Pacific coast salmon you buy in a store and pay three or four or five dollars a pound for.

There are also brook trout and rainbow in the lake. Fishermen say the rainbow are the most fun to catch but the salmon are the best tasting.

Ice fishing has its good days and its bad days. A good day for fishermen is when the fish bite fast and furiously. A good day for bystanders like me is when the wind is not blowing a gale, when the air is not too cold, and when the sun is shining bright.

Then the sky is blue as a forget-me-not and the air is so clear you want to bottle it and take it home. It might not be a bad idea. A friend of mine has a can labeled "Smog from Southern California." Why not a jug of "Pure Mountain Air," with the directions, "Breathe when needed."

I walked across the lake with my face in the sun, getting my vitamin D and feeling virtuous because I'd just read in a magazine how much better vitamin D is if you can get it from the sun instead of from pills.

The wind was at my back, the sun was on my face, and I looked at the dark green pine trees on the shore of the lake and thought of the stories I've read about the oldtime TB sanitariums in Switzerland. Didn't people sit on the balconies of those snow-covered chalets—protected from the wind by glass partitions but letting the sun touch as much of their skin as possible? With our modern clothing we don't suffer from the cold. We can let the sun touch our faces even at zero temperatures.

The snow was packed into a hard crust. I had no trouble walking on it. The day was very quiet because it was not a weekend. There were no snowmobiles sputtering, very few cars went by, the fishermen were quietly going about their business, sitting or standing on the ice. From across the lake they looked like gnomes peering into the underworld.

We ate one of each kind of fish for supper: Kokanee, brook, rainbow, then froze the rest in milk cartons.

I won't keep them too long. I have plans for salmon souffle, poached salmon, salmon and black olive salad, and creamed salmon on toast. And every time I serve one of these dishes, I will remember the cold, pure mountain air.

Lentil Cheese Bake

It was our last New Year's Eve in Chile and I stopped by the home of my friend Ruth, who worked in the United Nations Santiago bureau. It was a beautiful moonlit midsummer night and we were sitting in Ruth's garden when the housekeeper came with a saucedish of lentils for each of us. I must have looked as puzzled as I felt, because Ruth said, "Maria insists on this. It's for good luck in the new year."

Right here in Montana last year my friend Nancy came with a dish of black-eyed peas.

Somewhere I read that Japanese families gather on New Year's Eve to dine on buckwheat noodles. (Maybe this was in the old days.) Anyway, we know that people gather on New Year's Eve and we know that many gatherings these days are potluck. Lentil Cheese Bake is a casserole you could take to a New Year's potluck.

1 medium onion, chopped

3 tablespoons oil

1⅓ cups lentils

4 cups water

1 rib celery, chopped

¼ teaspoon summer savory

pinch of thyme

1 cup grated carrot

1 medium-sized potato, diced

1 teaspoon salt

2 tablespoons powdered skim milk mixed into 4 tablespoons water

½ cup grated cheese

In a heavy saucepan, saute onion in oil. Add lentils, stir to coat with oil. Add water, celery, savory and thyme. Bring to boil, cover, and simmer for 45 minutes.

Add carrot, potato and salt. Simmer 10 minutes. Stir in milk and ¼ cup grated cheese. Empty mixture into greased casserole. Bake, covered, in a preheated 350° oven for 30 minutes.

Remove cover. Sprinkle remaining ¼ cup of cheese on top of lentil mixture and return to oven until cheese is melted. If you wish your cheese browned, use the broiler.

Serves four.

No Sugar Baked Beans

You don't have to rely on sugar or molasses to flavor baked beans. I've been to potlucks where all the beans tasted like dessert. This recipe relies on apples, winter squash (high in vitamin A as well as natural sweetness) and good beans.

3 cups cooked pinto beans*

2 tablespoons oil

½ cup chopped onion

1 cup 1-inch cubes of raw winter squash

3 medium apples, finely chopped

¼ cup tomato paste

1 teaspoon salt

¼ teaspoon dried basil

1 cup (or more) water in which beans were cooked

In a skillet, saute onion in oil for 3 minutes. Add winter squash, apples, tomato paste, salt, basil and 1 cup bean liquid. Simmer, covered, for 10 minutes.

Add beans and heat to boiling. Pour into beanpot. Bake, covered, in preheated 300° oven for 30 minutes. Uncover and bake 30 minutes more. Add more bean liquid, or water if beans become dry.

Serves four.

*See page 50 for instructions for cooking beans.

Feijoada *(Brazilian Black Bean Stew)*

Feijoada is a Brazilian peasant dish. You don't find it on the menu in a Copacabana tourist hotel. The original version has ingredients such as salted dried pig's ears and pig's knuckles. I've eaten that version, went out of my way to eat it in a small cafe in Belem, Brazil. I've revised the recipe to fit our American diet.

1 pound dried black beans

6 cups cold water

6 cups warm water

5 cups warm water

1 small smoked beef or pork tongue

½ pound pork loin, in one piece

1 pound smoked sausage, in links

4 ounces ham, cubed

1 large onion, chopped

2 cloves garlic, chopped

2 large tomatoes, diced

2 tablespoons chopped parsley

¼ teaspoon crushed dried red chili peppers

Wash beans. Place them in a large pot with 6 cups cold water. Bring to a boil and boil for 2 minutes. Cover and let stand ½ hour. Drain.

Add 6 cups warm water, cover and simmer ½ hour. Drain.

Add 5 cups warm water and tongue. Simmer, covered, 1 hour. Add pork loin, smoked sausage and ham. Simmer, covered, ½ hour. Remove tongue. Skin the tongue and return it to pot.

Remove 1 cup beans and mash them. Return beans to pot. Add onion, garlic, tomato, parsley and crushed chili peppers. Add warm water if needed. Simmer 40 minutes. Beans should be tender and stew should be thick. Keep a close watch to make sure the stew doesn't burn.

When ready to serve, lift out the meat, carve it and arrange it on a platter. Serve beans in a soup tureen.

Serve with steamed rice and steamed swiss chard. Have on the table a bottle of hot chili pepper sauce and a plate of orange slices.

Serves ten to twelve.

Arroz con Pollo (Rice with Chicken)

This is a Spanish dish, but variations of it are so well known one hardly needs to translate the name. My mother made rice with chicken and we thought it was Hungarian. I went to Chile and I thought it was Chilean. Rice with chicken is just a good, satisfying combination.

1 small chicken, cut up

2 tablespoons oil

1 cup chopped onion

1 clove garlic, minced

1¼ cups uncooked rice

2 tomatoes, diced

1 rib celery, diced

1 small jar green olives

¼ teaspoon saffron (optional because it's expensive)

½ teaspoon salt

1 tablespoon fresh cilantro leaves (coriander)

2½ cups hot water

1 canned pimento, diced

Brown the chicken in oil in a heavy saucepan. Remove it from the pan, and saute onion, garlic and rice in the same pan. Add tomatoes, celery, olives, saffron, salt, cilantro, hot water and the chicken. Simmer, covered, until chicken and rice are tender. Add pimento just before serving.
Serves four.

The Pass Is Closed

The pass was a swirl of snow. We couldn't see two feet in front of us. We had to stop the car and wait for an opening. It came and we went over the top but it was scary. The next day the radio said, "Pass closed."

I don't think I will ever get over the tingle that goes up and down my spine at those words, "the pass is closed."

What is a pass to an easterner or a southerner? Well, remember that movie "Seven Brides for Seven Brothers?" The seven brothers kidnapped seven young women and took them home to their ranch. Of course the families of the young women pursued them. But Chung! an avalanche of snow rolled down the mountain between the pursuers and the pursued. The pass was closed. What did that mean? It meant that the opening between two mountain peaks was not open any more. The road was closed by a heap of snow. And it stayed closed all winter. Then one day came the magic words "the pass is open." The chase between the pursued and the pursuers went on.

In the West we still use the magic words "the pass is open." Ah, we can go, we can do. Or "the pass is closed." Can't go, can't do, stay home.

There's something mysterious about a pass, at least there is to me. It's like an unknown quantity. You can be going along in more or less equable weather. The highway is open, the skies are clear and then you come to a sign that says "CHAIN UP." You stop and put on your chains, or at least stop and hold a conference. Then you go on and suddenly you are in a very unpredictable climate. It can be the same as down below or it can be the opposite. Generally it is worse. Wind howling, snow piling up, hail pelleting down, or all of these together and the visibility is nil.

One way or another you get over the pass. When you arrive home the first question you are asked is "How was the pass?" You answer and for a moment all activity stops. A faraway look comes on everyone's face. You can see the awe on the faces—just momentary but it's there. Even in this Height-of-Technology era the pass may—or may not—be open.

You don't say it but you think it: there are forces left in this world that are still unconquered. Good for you!

Hungarian Goulash

We'd never heard of any kind of meat except what is now called organic when I grew up on a rock hill farm in upper New York state. Meat was lean, often rather tough, but it had flavor and nobody thought about such a thing as chemical residue.

I still prefer grassfed beef. Actually, my husband and I eat mostly deer and elk meat. This recipe will work very well with wild meat.

Some people will say one pound of meat is not enough for four servings. You can use one and one half pounds if you like. My husband and I are not big meat eaters any longer.

1 pound round steak, cut in 1-inch cubes

2 tablespoons oil

1 cup diced onion

1 teaspoon Hungarian paprika (use ½ teaspoon if you use ordinary paprika)

½ teaspoon salt

dash of pepper

¾ cup tomato juice, heated to boiling

1 tablespoon flour

2 tablespoons water

½ cup sour cream or yogurt

sprinkle of parsley

In a heavy pot, brown meat on both sides in hot oil. Remove meat. Saute onion until it is transparent. Stir in paprika and fry 2 minutes, being careful not to burn it. Return meat to pot. Add salt, pepper, tomato juice. Simmer, covered, until meat is tender. Add more tomato juice as needed to keep meat from scorching.

Remove meat from pot and thicken gravy with 1 tablespoon flour mixed in 2 tablespoons of cold water.

Stir ½ cup of the hot gravy into the sour cream (or yogurt). Return to pot. Return meat to pot. Stir. Heat thoroughly but do not boil. Sprinkle parsley on top.

Serve on noodles. Whole wheat or spinach noodles are good.

Serves four.

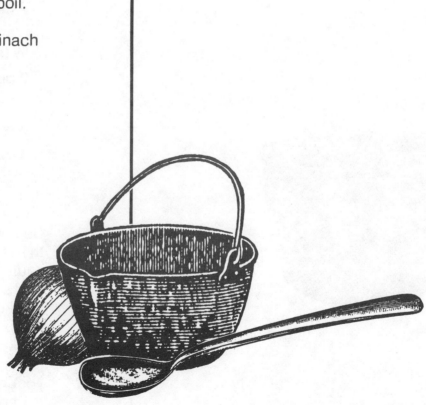

Chicken Paprika

My mother made this from an old hen that didn't lay any more. We had to cook it for hours. But I prefer that kind of chicken. It ate real corn and real wheat. It even ate earthworms.

a 3-pound chicken, cut into pieces

2 tablespoons oil

1 cup chopped onion

½ clove garlic

2 tablespoons Hungarian paprika (use 1 tablespoon if using ordinary paprika)

½ teaspoon salt

3 cups water

1 tablespoon flour

3 tablespoons milk

1 cup sour cream or yogurt

In a heavy pot, brown chicken in oil. Remove from pot. Saute onion and garlic in the same pot for 3 minutes. Add paprika and saute 1 minute longer. Return chicken to pot. Add salt and water. Simmer, covered, until chicken is tender.

Mix flour with milk. Add it to the pot and cook 5 minutes. Remove 1 cup hot gravy from pot and mix gently into sour cream (or yogurt). Return to pot. Heat but do not boil.

Serve on noodles, preferably whole wheat. Serves four.

Christmas Is A Connection

I went to visit a friend and I heard loud banging in her attic. "What's going on?" I asked. "That's my Christmas present," Julie said. "My neighbor is putting insulation in my attic. I bought the insulation and I wanted to pay him for installing it but he said it was his Christmas present to me."

I like that idea. It fits in with the way the world is today. Many people don't have money to buy presents. I say OK, there's no law that says you have to exchange presents at Christmas. As a matter of fact, there's no law that says you have to observe Christmas at all. I have a confession to make. I have skipped many Christmases and the sky didn't fall.

It was one of the blessings of living in that upside down land of South America (upside down only to us foreigners) that Christmas came in summer. There were years Mel and I slipped quietly out of town and camped at a blue lake high in the Andes, as far away and remote as a soaring condor.

But we came back and made our connections. That's what I think Christmas is: it's a connection between people. But it doesn't have to be an exchange of expensive gifts. Mel and I gave that up years ago.

I have my friend Dotty in South America to thank for initiating me into the idea of exchanging homemade goodies. Every Christmas she came over to our house with a freshly baked German *stollen* and the traditional anise-flavored *springerle* cookies.

Of course some people would drop dead if you didn't buy them "things" for Christmas. Some people are definitely "things" people. I'm not. I just tell everyone, "I'm not into *things*."

I think everyone should do as her/his conscience bids. If you want to buy, go ahead and buy. The stores need the business. But if you don't want to buy, you don't have to feel guilty about it. It is now accepted. You can simply smile at your friends and neighbors and say "Merry Christmas" and that's that.

But if you want to do a favor, and you have the time, that's very fine too. Along with the smile and the "Merry Christmas"—that's the real connection.

Now that Mel and I are back in Montana where Christmas comes in winter, we like the warmth of a shared Christmas: people coming together with food, talk, laughter, song.

Elk Roast with Horseradish Sauce

Mel and I often cook an elk roast for Christmas. I don't feel we have to be tied to turkey or goose. My Hungarian parents didn't have that tradition. I remember having roast pork or roast chicken.

Mel and I have started our own tradition. For us roast elk is as good as roast beef. Maybe better—certainly it's lean and grassfed.

I call our way of cooking the elk *nouvelle cuisine elk roast*. *Nouvelle cuisine* of course refers to the newer style of French cooking—the lower calorie way—in contrast to the old way of putting rich sauces on everything.

A lot of game recipes call for that same type of rich sauce. That's fine if you like it, but my husband and I have found that you can treat a good cut of elk as if it were first class roast beef.

a 3-pound elk roast

5 cloves garlic

sprinkling of pepper

Insert cloves of garlic in roast, poking the holes with the tip of a knife. Dust with pepper. Insert meat thermometer.

Place meat in a roasting pan, uncovered, in preheated 350° oven. After 35 minutes lower the temperature to 300° and cook until the meat thermometer reads the desired degree of doneness, about 20 minutes to the pound.

Remove from the oven. Let stand 5 minutes before carving. Serve with horseradish sauce.

Serves eight.

Horseradish Sauce

1 cup yogurt

1 teaspoon white vinegar

1 tablespoon grated fresh horseradish (or 1½ tablespoons prepared horseradish)

1 teaspoon prepared mustard

1 tablespoon chopped chives

1 tablespoon mayonnaise (use 2 tablespoons if yogurt is non-fat)

Mix ingredients.
Makes 1¼ cups.

Montana Stuffed Baked Trout

The first stuffed baked trout I ever ate was a Christmas celebration in the Andes Mountains, on the border between Chile and Argentina. Mel and I were on a camping-fishing vacation. December is summer in South America.

Mel caught the fish in a mountain lake, cleaned it, stuffed it with bread, onion and herb stuffing, rolled it in wet newspapers (we didn't have aluminum foil in those days), and laid it on a bed of red-hot coals.

What a feast that was! We drank red Chilean wine and watched the sun set behind a grove of monkey-puzzle trees.

We also took trout home and baked them for our friends. Now that we're back in Montana we use the same recipe for Montana trout.

a 2 or 3-pound trout, cleaned

4 or 5 slices medium dry bread, hand crumbled (about 2 cups)

2 tablespoons butter

¾ cup tender celery, chopped

1 medium onion, chopped

1 tablespoon green onion, chopped

2 tablespoons chopped parsley

¼ teaspoon black pepper

½ teaspoon sage

½ teaspoon basil

Wash trout and pat dry with a paper towel. Sprinkle with salt and pepper inside and out.

Saute celery and onion in butter for 5 minutes, then mix with other ingredients. Stuff the fish lightly with dressing. If there is leftover dressing put it in a baking dish, add a few drops of water, cover, and bake along with the fish. (Fish dressing should be dry as it absorbs moisture from the fish while baking, and will become pasty if water is added beforehand.)

Bake fish and dressing in preheated 350° oven for about 40 minutes. Serve with lemon wedges.

Serves four to six.

Recycling Christmas Cards

I did it. I recycled a Christmas card: cut off the front, glued it on a folded piece of paper and wrote inside. Now before I tell you why I did it, I want to say I don't advocate everyone going around recycling Christmas cards. It's not good for the economy, and it's not good for original artists who make cards one by one and have to sell enough around the holidays to live on the rest of the year.

But there are cases when recycling Christmas cards is the only thing to do. If you can barely afford the twenty cents to pay the postage, then go right ahead and don't be bashful. Take your pen and write on the cards, "This is a recycled Christmas card. Merry Christmas, Happy New Year."

I learned this in South America. The charity organizations were doing it. They put new backing on old cards and sold them to raise money. They even made the envelopes. They unglued an old envelope to get the pattern.

Some Christmas cards are simply too beautiful to throw away. Or they fit a certain occasion absolutely perfectly. That's the way it was with this card I just recycled. It had a mother deer and two fawns on it and there was a willow tree. Well, this friend of mine had two fawns born in her garden under a willow tree. They weren't born at the same time; that's when the adventure started. Jean was walking in her garden, and she heard a bleating like a lamb. A fawn came out from under the willow tree and followed Jean. Jean waved her arms. "Go away!" she yelled. She knew she mustn't touch the fawn. It was only an hour or so old, but Jean was afraid it would cross the road and get hit by a car. An hour-old fawn doesn't know enough to be afraid of humans—at least this one didn't. It kept on following Jean. She had to run away because the fawn wouldn't.

Jean knew the fawn's mother was probably on the edge of the woods watching and would come right down and teach the fawn a lesson. But it turned out the mother deer was giving birth to another fawn.

Jean saw the doe and the two fawns all summer. In fact, she saw too much of those three deer. They ate up half her garden. Actually, Jean didn't mind too much. As she said, "They're part of my acreage. They come out of the woods into the field, and if I put a garden into the field, well, I have to expect to feed some deer."

That year Jean put a high fence around her garden, but the deer jumped right over. This year she put chicken wire flat on the ground, and the deer seem to think twice before crossing it. They still eat some corn and beans, but there's enough to go around.

Anyway, Jean is going to receive this recycled Christmas card with a mother deer, two fawns and a willow tree.

I'd probably recycle a lot more cards, but I have a big supply of new cards I bought at a rummage sale. Well, they're not really new—they're about five years old. One of them says that a novena is being said in your behalf by the missionaries in the South Pacific, and it's dated 1976. I won't send that one because it wouldn't be proper. But the rest are good ordinary cards.

I always put a letter in my cards, so I feel the picture doesn't have to be world-shaking. The purpose of Christmas cards is for people to reach out and touch each other. It doesn't matter if a card is recycled or if it's a leftover. It still makes the connection. "I'm thinking of you. Merry Christmas. Happy New Year."

Empanadas *(Chilean Meat Turnovers)*

Empanadas will always be connected to a South American Christmas for me because Mel and I would stop at a bakery on our way out of town—to the mountains or wherever we were going—and buy two of these meat pies hot from the oven. We each ate one as we drove along and it was a complete meal.

Eating an *empanada* in Chile was like waving the flag. On the Chilean national day—their 4th of July—if you didn't have an *empanada* in your hand your name was mud.

In the city the *empanadas* were baked in regular ovens, but in the country they were baked in an outdoor clay oven, and the fuel could be blackberry vines. Not skinny little canes, but large fat ones. The blackberry, which was introduced into Chile to be friendly, turned into an enemy which threatens to take over the southern half of the country.

Basically the *empanada* is not too different from a Butte pasty, that Cornish meat pie which was traditionally carried in miners' lunch buckets.

I use an up-to-date Chilean recipe for the *empanadas*. It uses baking powder in the dough.

3½ cups all-purpose flour

2 teaspoons baking powder

½ cup lard (or vegetable shortening)

1 egg yolk, slightly beaten

¼ cup white wine

1 teaspoon salt

¾ cup hot milk

1 recipe meat filling (see below)

12 purple olives

24 raisins

3 hardcooked eggs

1 whole egg, beaten

Sift flour and baking powder. Cut in lard as you would for a pie crust. Add egg yolk and wine. Mix well.

Dissolve salt in hot milk, and add to flour mixture. Mix with hands into a soft dough. Do not knead. Just mix gently until the dough is smooth. Work rapidly so dough does not get cold. Place dough in warmed bowl, cover with warmed cloth and let it sit for 15 minutes.

Divide dough into 12 equal parts. Roll one by one into circles, about 6 inches across and about the thickness of pie crust. On each circle place 1 large spoonful of meat filling, 1 olive, 2 raisins and a slice of hardcooked egg. Fold circle in half so it is a half-moon shape. Wet edges with water and seal. Turn corner edges of half-moon up. Paint tops with beaten egg.

Bake in preheated 375° oven on an ungreased cookie sheet about 30 minutes. Don't open the oven for the first 15 minutes.

Makes 12 *empanadas*.

Meat Filling

½ pound lean ground beef

1¼ cups finely chopped onion

2 tablespoons oil

5 tablespoons hot water

1 teaspoon paprika

pinch of ground dried chili peppers

½ teaspoon oregano

¼ teaspoon ground cumin

½ teaspoon salt

1 tablespoon flour

3 tablespoons cold water

In a skillet saute meat and onion in oil. Add hot water, spices and salt. Cover and simmer for 30 minutes.

Mix flour with cold water and add to meat mixture. Cook 3 minutes. Set aside until *empanadas* are ready to be filled.

Pebre *(South American Hot Sauce)*

Some *empanadas* are made with hot chili pepper in the filling. Others are made without the chili pepper in the filling but are served with hot sauce on the side.

Eating chilies is quite foreign to many North American palates. My husband and I were introduced to this custom in South America. At first my mouth fell open at the sight of people eating fresh green chili peppers like I would eat sweet bell peppers: sliced open, seeds removed (they are even hotter than the flesh), then the long thin halves chewed and swallowed. My friend Celia ate chilies laid on a buttered roll. My mouth watered at the sight.

Chilies don't seem to be harmful to one's health. In fact, they seem to promote health. My Latin friends swore chili peppers toned up their digestion. My own husband has been eating them for thirty years.

I've found scientific evidence to back up a statement that adding hot peppers to a hot soup when you have a cold will ease your discomfort. This doubly hot soup won't cure your cold, but it will warm you up. It will make you perspire, and if you go to bed and perspire, your aching joints will feel better.

I can't eat chilies laid on a slice of bread but I can eat them in hot chicken soup or in this *pebre* sauce. In fact, I like *pebre* sauce just as well as I like horseradish sauce. They are very different but both are good.

1 cup chopped tomato

2 tablespoons chopped onion

1 tablespoon fresh cilantro leaves (coriander)

2 hot green chili peppers, seeded and chopped

Mix all ingredients and the *pebre* is ready to eat. Store leftover sauce in refrigerator in a jar or bowl with a tight-fitting lid. It keeps only a day or two.

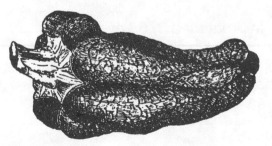

"Witch's Brew Won't Do" New Year's Punch

My New Year's Punch is for the teetotalers in the crowd—although you can add alcohol if you want. It's for the kind of party where all ages are present: children, teenagers, middle-aged people and senior citizens.

I like that kind of party. It reminds me of our days in South America where the generations were all together.

I hesitated before putting this recipe down in black and white. The base is sour cherry juice, which is fine, but do I dare tell that these cherries have worms in them? You know how sour cherries (pie cherries) are. They get worms if the trees aren't sprayed. At least they do in my neighborhood. So people are more than willing to give these cherries away. Every year I get boxes and boxes.

Sometimes I sit down and pit the cherries and remove the little worms (they're perfectly innocuous little worms) and make a pie or jam.

But after I'm tired of all that I take the rest of the cherries and make fruit juice. I boil the cherries, pits and all, and then strain them through a jellybag.

The juice is lovely—amber pink in color and it has a good consistency. It has body to it. Now don't say "Of course it has body—it has bodies!" I strain the juice very well and don't forget—it was boiled ten minutes. *Skoal!*

1 quart canned sour cherry juice (unsweetened)

1 cinnamon stick about 2 inches long

3 whole cloves

1 quart apple cider

1 can (12 oz.) frozen orange juice concentrate

1 quart water

honey for sweetening, if desired

Simmer sour cherry juice, cinnamon stick and cloves 10 minutes. Cool. Pour into a punch bowl. Add apple cider, orange juice concentrate, water and ice cubes. Float an orange slice on top.

Makes three quarts.

Kalács (Hungarian Christmas Bread)

The smell of the kitchen when my mother made this holiday bread is something that will stay with me the rest of my life. It's the smell of Christmas: a warm sweet yeast bread, creamy yellow, light as a feather, swirled with cinnamon and nuts.

Put on the kettle, sit down around the kitchen table, and slice the *kalács*. You need the whole family—the whole neighborhood—to smell the *kalács*, to taste it, to savor it.

I think almost every ethnic group makes a Christmas bread. The Germans have *stollen,* the Italians have *panettone*. There is the braided *vanocka*. There is Scandinavian coffee cake. The ingredients are much alike.

I've compared my mother's Hungarian bread with the Chilean holiday bread, which was called *Pan de Pascua*—literally "bread of Easter"—but it was baked for Christmas too. The Chilean bread was made with the same basic dough of flour, eggs, butter, sugar, milk and yeast, but the flavoring was different. The Chilean holiday bread has an anise flavor. One recipe I have calls for ¼ teaspoon ground anise seeds.

The idea for all these breads is the same. You offer guests a slice of freshly baked holiday bread. And when you are invited to a holiday get-together, you stop by a bakery and buy a loaf wrapped in holiday paper.

The Chilean *Pan de Pascua* is always a round loaf. My mother's *kalács* could be a round loaf or it could be baked in a tube pan so it has a hole in the middle.

1 cup milk

½ cup butter or margarine

¼ cup lukewarm water

1 tablespoon dry yeast (or 1 package)

3 cups flour

½ cup sugar

1 teaspoon salt

2 eggs, beaten

grated rind of 1 lemon

⅓ cup halved red candied cherries

½ cup raisins (golden)

⅓ cup citron

2 cups flour or more

sugar and cinnamon

Heat milk and butter in saucepan until just blended. Cool to lukewarm. Put yeast into ¼ cup water and let stand with 1 teaspoon sugar until dissolved (10 minutes). Combine yeast and butter mixture.

Sift flour, sugar and salt into a warm bowl. Add lukewarm butter mixture. Beat hard with wooden spoon. Add eggs, and the rest of the flour. Knead for 8-10 minutes until dough is elastic and clears from the bowl and hands. Add fruit and knead another minute or two.

Grease another bowl and warm it in the oven. Turn dough into it until all sides are greased. Cover with waxed paper and clean lightweight towel. Let rise in oven (with heat off, at 80°) until double in bulk, 2-2½ hours.

Turn onto a floured board. Knead a few strokes, then flatten to about 1-inch thickness. Sprinkle with 2 tablespoons sugar mixed with ¼ teaspoon cinnamon. Roll up and put into an angel food or tube pan, or lay on a flat baking sheet. Let rise 1½ hours or until double in bulk. Brush with melted butter. Sprinkle with another 2 tablespoons sugar and ½ teaspoon cinnamon.

Bake 45 minutes at 350°.

Kim's mother's recipe as adapted by Kim's sister, Froni Kandiko Crane

Kalacs (ka-LÁ-cha) is defined in a Hungarian dictionary as ''cake.''

Palacsínta (Hungarian Crepes)

Another favorite memory of my mother's holiday cooking is *Palacsinta*, which are a kind of cheese blintz. You could call *Palacsinta* crepes, but they aren't anything like a commercial crepe. The first time I ate a commercial crepe I flew to the typewriter and dashed off a letter to my mother.

"Dear Mom,

"What a disappointment! I went to a real *Palacsinta* place in Minneapolis. It was called a creperie. *Palacsinta* are crepes, or you can call them blintzes.

"I'm going to have a cheese blintz, I said—a real cheese blintz like that play I was in, *You Can't Take It With You*. I was the Grand Duchess Olga Katrina who used to be somebody in Russia and now was waiting tables at Child's. She was lamenting the cheese blintzes of her youth.

"Well, I'm lamenting them too. Here were all these people in this fancy creperie, making the crepes right under my nose, dipping the back of a frying pan into the batter, then one, two, three, back to the grill and one, two, three, off the frying pan into a basket.

"Very lovely—full of atmosphere—but there is no relation to food. Mom, these *Palacsinta* are as thin as paper and they taste like paper. Maybe that's what the customers want—just filling. But how can your stomach be happy with all filling and no outside?

"Mom, don't ever order a *Palacsinta* in a creperie. It's nothing but a disk of paper. I'm coming home. Heat up the frying pan."

1 - 3 eggs (the more eggs the more tender
    and delicate the crepe)

1 cup flour

1 tablespoon sugar

½ teaspoon salt

1 cup milk

melted shortening for greasing skillet

Beat the eggs. Stir flour, sugar and salt into eggs. Add milk, beating until you have a smooth creamy mixture.

Grease a 6-inch skillet and place over moderate heat. When a drop of batter sizzles upon being dropped into the skillet, pour in a ladle of batter (about 2½ tablespoons) and quickly tip skillet with a rotary motion so batter is spread evenly over entire surface. Cook a couple of minutes until crepe is firm—lightly browned underneath and just curling at the edges. Flip with a table knife run under the center of the crepe. Brown second side, then stack on a warm plate.

Greasing the skillet after the first crepe may not be necessary.

Filling

2 cups cottage cheese

¼ teaspoon cinnamon

1 tablespoon sugar

Mix all ingredients. Spread a heaping tablespoon over the top crepe of the stack and roll up. Lay filled crepe on a heatproof platter. Continue until all crepes are filled.

Place platter of crepes in oven and heat through. Serve plain or with a dab of raspberry jam, or a spoonful of fresh wild strawberries crushed with sugar.

Kim's mother's recipe as adapted by Kim's sister, Froni Kandiko Crane

Two Stage Diet

After the high eating of the holidays you have to come down to earth. You have to lose five pounds (or more). But don't lose community. You'll need to solace each other with Saturday Soup, Lean Cookies and Herb Tea.

Now this won't work for everyone, but I'm convinced the reason I lost my seven pounds is that I did it in two stages. I call this my two stage diet. You can try it if you like. During the first stage don't expect to lose an ounce. Oh, I know this sounds foolish. Anyone who goes on a diet wants to lose five pounds right then and there. I don't agree. I think the first thing to do is to get yourself in shape so you *can* go on a diet. More to the point—so the five or ten pounds you lose stay off. We all know people who have lost two hundred pounds but they're the same size they always were. The weight comes off but it goes right back on.

My theory is that people fall off their diets because their bodies are not in shape to stand the pressure. It takes strength to resist food. Eating is a solace, a companion. Sometimes it's the most interesting thing in one's day. To give that up you have to be very strong. Remember what I said a few years ago: the secret of dieting is to eat lightly and leave home. I meant fill your life with other interesting things besides food. Well, that still holds. Eat lightly and leave home.

But today I'm talking about the food you *do* eat. Stage one of my two stage diet is to eat all the food you want. "What!" you will say. Wait! Food as defined in this diet omits all junk food. It omits liquid protein and all that kind of stuff. I say for the body to withstand temptation it has to eat food—not drink it, not swallow it in pills—the body has to sit down and chew good solid food. And enough of it so that you don't have a hollow feeling in your middle.

Eat whole grain bread made from freshly ground whole grains. Eat that same kind of hot cereal. Eat plain roast meat, plain yogurt, plain cooked vegetables. I'm talking about people who have to change gradually.

You can even allow yourself cheese and nuts in stage one. The point is not to lose weight. It's to set the stage for losing weight later.

If you cut out junk food in stage one, but allow yourself all you want of plain good food, you won't have the cravings that throw you off your diet later. By now you've guessed what stage two of this diet is. It's to eat the same kind of food as in stage one but to cut down on the quantity. And you can do it because you've got a base to stand on. You've already cut out sugar, white flour, candy, doughnuts, ice cream, soda pop. I include diet drinks also. I don't think they help a bit in staying on a diet. Artificial foods produce peculiar cravings. You can't stay on a diet if your body has all sorts of cravings, if you could kill someone for a candy bar.

Stage one is to prepare your body so it isn't a bundle of raw nerves. What about coffee, tea and alcohol? Well, you can try the diet without cutting them out but I don't think stage two will work very well. When you cut down on the quantity of food, even good food, you can't have a lot of coffee, tea and alcohol sloshing around in an empty stomach. I'd say the thing to drink would be a mild herb tea.

I allowed a whole month in stage one. And you know what happened? I started losing weight before I even got to stage two.

Peanut Buttery Cereal

My breakfast has to be a hot cereal—and not just any old hot cereal. Our friend Larry came by the other day and he said, "I've got my shelf full of hot cereals and I don't like any of them." They're probably stale from being two years in the box.

I'll give him some farm wheat freshly ground. He can cook it and eat it with a banana on top. I love a sliced banana on hot cereal. Try it some time. No sugar—just a sliced banana and whole milk.

If you want to tempt kids, add a little peanut butter to the pot while you're cooking the cereal. Real peanut butter—the old-fashioned kind. It makes the cereal creamy and rich. You can go all morning without feeling hungry.

1 cup rolled oats

½ cup rolled wheat

2 tablespoons bulgur wheat

4 ¼ cups water

1 cup powdered skim milk

½ teaspoon salt

2 tablespoons peanut butter

Mix milk powder with water and salt. Bring it to a boil in the top of a double boiler placed directly on the heat. Add cereals. Cook, stirring constantly, for 2 minutes. Put boiling water in bottom of double boiler and replace top. Cover.

Cook slowly for 30 minutes over moderate heat. Add peanut butter. Stir well. Serve with low-fat milk.

Serves four.

Rose Hip Tea

Rose hip tea has been famous for centuries. Some people consider it their source of vitamin C. Rose hips—the red-orange fruits of rose bushes—are very high in vitamin C. Of course, how much of the vitamin actually ends up in your tea cup depends on many factors: the variety of rose, the care taken of the fruit after it was picked, the length of time it was stored. Vitamin C is perishable.

I would say that frozen rose hips retain the most vitamin C; canned—second; dried—third. I've read charts of tests made on dried rose hips. Some batches had high amounts; some had very little.

I dry my own rose hips. I pick them in an area that has not been sprayed. I wash them carefully, remove stem and blossom ends, then dry them in the shade. I store rose hips (as I do all herbs) in an airtight container inside a cupboard, away from bright light. This way of storing preserves the fragrance of herbs and as much of the vitamin value as is possible.

You can make rose hip tea in three ways: using a canned puree (see recipe page 97), using frozen rose hips (I freeze a quart or two of rose hips every year), or using dried rose hips.

If using canned puree, all you need for tea is a tablespoon of puree, a mug of hot water and honey to taste.

The following recipe is for tea made from frozen or dried rose hips.

¼ cup rose hips, dried or frozen

1 good-sized piece of dried orange peel

1 small piece of cinnamon stick

1 quart hot water

If using dried rose hips, break them up as finely as possible before placing in teapot. I sometimes have to put the rose hips in a paper sack and pound on them with a hammer. Frozen hips, of course, defrost and become soft. Pour the hot water over the rose hips in a teapot. Frozen hips can now be mashed with a wooden spoon. Let steep 10-15 minutes. Strain. If necessary, reheat gently before serving. Do not boil as boiling destroys some vitamin C.

Add the orange peel and cinnamon stick.
Makes four cups.

Family Carrot Cake

They say without a song the day would never end. Well, without a carrot cake a healthful cookbook cannot be terminated. This recipe comes from my mother-in-law. I cut down a bit on the amount of sugar.

1½ **cups grated carrot**

1 **cup raisins**

¾ **cup sugar or** ½ **cup honey**

¼ **cup shortening**

1 **teaspoon cinnamon**

1 **teaspoon nutmeg**

1⅓ **cups water**

1 **egg, beaten until light**

½ **teaspoon grated lemon rind**

2 **cups sifted flour (1 cup whole wheat, and 1 cup white if you like)**

1 **teaspoon baking soda**

1 **teaspoon cream of tartar**

½ **teaspoon salt**

½ **cup chopped walnuts**

Cook the carrots, raisins, sugar, shortening, cinnamon and nutmeg in 1⅓ cups water for 5 minutes. Allow the mixture to cool for 2-3 hours.

Stir the beaten egg into the cooled mixture. Add lemon rind.

In a separate bowl, sift together the flour, baking soda, cream of tartar and salt. Stir into carrot mixture until well blended. Add nuts.

Pour into a greased 9 x 13 pan. Bake 35-45 minutes (or until done) in a preheated 350° oven.

This cake does not need frosting. If you must adorn it, sprinkle lightly with confectioner's sugar.

Index